D1549497

**Wakefield Libraries
& Information Services**

19 JAN 2004	-5 OCT 2005
	21 JUN 2008
	31 JAN 2011
LANZER	22/2/16
French	
Pbk	
J448.076	-7 MAR 2015
£4.99 AS	31 OCT 2015
	OSSETT LIBRARY STATION ROAD OSSETT WAKEFIELD WF5 8AB 01924 303040

This book should be returned by the last date stamped
above. You may renew the loan personally, by post or
telephone for a further period if the book is not required by
another reader.

ench

te Lanzer

056 346 123 341 01

WAKEFIELD LIBRARIES & INFORMATION SERVICES	
Askews	28-Nov-2002
	£4.99

Published by BBC Educational Publishing, BBC White City,
201 Wood Lane, London W12 7TS
First published 1998, Reprinted 1999, Reprinted 2000, Reprinted 2001
© Harriette Lanzer/BBC Worldwide (Educational Publishing) 1998
Photographs: © Honsingers

ISBN: 0 563 46123 3
All rights reserved. No part of this publication may be reproduced,
stored in any form or by any means mechanical, electronic,
photocopying, recording or otherwise without prior permission of
the publisher.

Designed by Ennismore Design.
Printed in Great Britain by Bell and Bain, Glasgow.

InfoZONE

(📺) These instructions might well appear in your exam, so see if you can try and learn them!

C'est vrai?   *Is it true?*

C'est faux?   *Is it wrong?*

Choisis/Choisissez.   *Choose.*

Choisis/Choisissez un des thèmes.
Choose one of the topics.

Coche la bonne case.
Tick the appropriate box.

Coche six cases.   *Tick six boxes.*

Complète/Completez les phrases/la grille.
Complete the sentences/grid.

Décris/Décrivez.   *Describe.*

Demande/Demandez.   *Ask.*

Dessine/Dessinez.   *Draw.*

Dis/Dites.   *Say.*

Donne/Donnez les détails sur ...
Give information about ...

Donne ton/Donnez votre avis sur ...
Give your opinion on ...

Ecoute/Ecoutez.   *Listen.*

Ecris/Ecrivez.   *Write.*

Ecris/Ecrivez la réponse.   *Write the answer.*

Ecris/Ecrivez les lettres/les numéros.
Write the letters/numbers.

Ecris/Ecrivez les noms corrects sur la carte.
Write the correct names on the map.

En français/anglais.   *In French/English.*

Entoure/Entourez oui ou non.
Draw a circle around yes or no.

Explique/Expliquez.   *Explain.*

Fais/Faites correspondre.   *Match.*

Fais/Faites des notes.   *Make notes.*

Fais/Faites une liste.   *Write a list.*

Lis/Lisez (l'article).   *Read the article.*

Ou ... ou ...   *Either ... or ...*

Pose/Posez des questions sur ...
Ask questions about ...

Que signifient les symboles?
What do the symbols mean?

Raconte/Racontez.   *Tell.*

Range/Rangez les phrases/images dans le bon
ordre.   *Put the sentences/pictures in
the right order.*

Regarde/Regardez ...   *Look at ...*

Relie/Reliez.   *Match.*

Remplis/Remplissez le formulaire/la grille.
Fill in the form/grid.

Remplis/Remplissez les blancs.
Fill in the gaps.

Réponds/Répondez (aux questions).
Answer (the questions).

Souligne/Soulignez.   *Underline.*

Trouve/Trouvez les mots.   *Find the words.*

Voilà un exemple.   *Here's an example.*

Quand?   *When?*

Pourquoi?   *Why?*

Où?   *Where?*

Que?   *What?*

Qu'est-ce que ...?   *What?*

Qui?   *Who?*

Comment?   *How?/What ... like?*

Combien?   *How much?*

Est-ce que ...?   *Is it so ...?*

Quel/quelle?   *Which?*

Some exam boards use the *tu* form for
instructions (*écoute/dis*) and others use the
vous form (*écoutez/dites*).

Contents

The World of Work 60

The International World 76

6

About BITESIZEfrench

BITESIZEfrench is a revision guide that has been specially put together to help you with your GCSE exams. You can watch the TV programmes, work your way through the activities and suggestions in this book and even call up the internet on-line service – whenever you choose.

It's called BITESIZEfrench because that's a good way to do your revision – in bitesize pieces, and not in one great chunk a few days before your exam! You can watch the video programmes whenever and as often as you want, and the book is divided up into small sections that you can go through one-by-one. Whenever you get stuck on anything or are feeling worried about a specific point, you can turn to the on-line team who are there to help you.

❶ REMEMBER This book aims to help you improve your mark in the exam. It gives you the basics you need to know for GCSE, but you'll also need to revise from your classwork, so check with your teacher that you're revising everything you should!

About this book

This book is divided into five sections, covering your key GCSE exam topics:
   Everyday Activities, including school, daily routine, health and food
   Personal and Social Life, including families and hobbies
   The World Around Us, including places in town, weather and shopping
   The World of Work, including jobs and phone calls
   The International World, including tourism and the environment.

Each of the sections in the book follows the same pattern, starting with an introduction to the topic plus a page of French phrases with their English translations (**InfoZONE**). These are key phrases so try to learn them.

Next, you'll find listening activities – these are based on the TV programmes, so make sure that you've got them all safely on video. You can listen to the video and rewind, fast forward, pause and stop it as often as you like – you're revising here and not being tested, so you can suit yourself for once.

Speaking activities come next. You can do these on your own and record them to use at a later date to revise from. Or you could do the activities with a friend from your French class and help each other with pronunciation!

You'll find reading activities next – you don't have to do them all at once though! Just take them bit-by-bit at your own pace.

Writing activities form the final part of each section, but you don't need to do them last of all. You can pick and choose any activities to do as you like. Tick each activity off and write the date by each one once you've done it. You might even like to repeat an activity a few weeks later to see how much you've remembered.

KEY TO SYMBOLS
📺 A link to the video
⑦ A suggestion to do
◎ An activity to do
ⓗ A Higher activity – ask your teacher if you need to do these.

Each section is full of advice and tips (**Remember!**) to help you as you work towards the big day of your exam, but feel free to jot down your own notes in the margins as well. There are also checklists throughout the book to help you keep a check on your revision progress.

If you're keen to revise some grammar before the exam, there are some grammar activities you can work on (**GrammarZONE**) and at the end of the book, you'll find the answers to most of the activities.

Planning your revision

When are your GCSE French exams? (Remember, you've got a speaking, listening, reading and a writing exam to think about.) Next month? Next year? Or tomorrow?! Well, the first thing you need to do is write down today's date. Then write down the date of your exams. How many days are there to go? Let's imagine that you've got 90 days. There are five sections in this book and on the video. So, let's divide 90 days by five sections. That's 18 days per section – nearly three weeks. But you've also got other subjects to revise for, so you can't spend all your time on French. Each of the sections has got 16 or 18 pages, so that works out at about one page per day for 90 days. Do you think you can manage that? Or would you prefer to do three pages a day and complete your revision in 30 days? It's up to you how you spread the revision out, but writing down an action plan for yourself will help you focus on what you need to do between now and the exam itself.

Once you've drawn up your revision timetable, you can start your actual work. When you revise, make sure that:
- you've got a quiet place to work
- you've got everything you need in the room – books, pens, paper, the video, a dictionary ...
- you don't get distracted by computer games, the TV, radio, magazines ...
- you don't revise for too long without a break – set a time limit for yourself to make sure that you keep fresh and motivated.

On the day

Make sure that you know the exact day, time and place for each of your French exams. Get to the exam room in good time and make sure that you've got a pen and a pencil with you. You might also like to take a ruler, a rubber, a dictionary (if your school isn't providing them) and a good luck mascot. On your way to the exam, go through a few key points in French – for instance, you could count to 50, say a bit about yourself or listen to a French cassette. There's not much point trying to learn new things in the few hours before the exam – so just concentrate on revising a bit to get yourself into a 'French' mood.

Nobody expects you to know everything on the day of your exam, but see if you can manage to do the following:
- check that you know the French instructions (page 3)
- say two or three sentences about yourself in French
- know your numbers to 50 (and above if possible)
- know some important key phrases (pages 9, 27, 45, 61, and 77).

Good luck with your revision – and good luck in your exam!

❗ REMEMBER Getting ready for an exam is like getting ready for a performance – the end result is you showing what you can do and making the most of what you know.

THE ON-LINE SERVICE
You can find extra support, tips and answers to your exam queries on the BITESIZE internet site. The address is http://www.bbc.co.uk/ education/revision

Everyday Activities

This section is about

- School

- Getting to school

- Your room

- Daily routine

- Health and fitness

- Food and drink

This section is all about everyday activities and that includes school, life at home, health and fitness and food. These are all topics that you'll need to know about for your exam.

In the exam, you'll be expected to be able to talk and write about the above topics. You'll also have to ask and understand questions on those topics. You can start off by beginning to identify key vocabulary you'll need – just look at page 9 for a start! You'll also have to give descriptions and details about these topics, so make sure you go into the exam well stocked with phrases!

Let's start with school (l'école) and the differences between French and British schools. Here are some interesting facts for you: School starts early in France – maybe even at ten to eight, but it finishes earlier too. French pupils don't have to wear a school uniform (l'uniforme scolaire), but they do have to do their homework (les devoirs) every day. And what are French pupils' favourite subjects (les matières préférées)? Well, you'll find out all about those in this section.

Once you've worked your way through the activities, you'll be able to describe your own school day too – and in your exam, you could well be asked to do just that!

And what about food in France? Well, the French really enjoy their food, so listen out for some specialities enjoyed by the pupils. French pupils can eat lunch (le déjeuner) at school in the canteen (à la cantine) so see how their menu compares with your school dinner! For breakfast (le petit déjeuner) you might get a croissant and a bowl of piping hot chocolate (le chocolat chaud) but you could probably also ask for cereal and milk (les céréales avec du lait) if that's what you really like in the morning! Can you say what you eat for breakfast? In French, that is! This sort of information is probably quite obvious to you – but remember that you'll need to be able to talk and write about it in French once you're in the exam.

Each section of this book starts off with an InfoZONE page – this lists words and phrases to do with the topics. It isn't a complete list of words you need to know for your exam, but it is a basic selection to start with. If you're a Higher level candidate, you'll need to know more words and phrases – your teacher will help you if you're unsure of what you need to know. Some of the phrases are just basic responses to questions, such as *Je vais par le train*. It's up to you to add to these and make your speech and writing more interesting!

So let's get started – allons-y!

◎ These phrases will be really useful for your exam, so see if you can try and learn them!

School subjects

Quelle est ta matière préférée?
  What's your favourite subject?

J'aime bien ...   I like ...

Ma matière préférée, c'est ...
  My favourite subject is ...

Mes matières préférées sont ... et ...
  My favourite subjects are ... and ...

l'anglais, le français, les maths, les sciences
  English, French, maths, science

l'histoire, la géographie, le sport, la musique
  history, geography, sport, music

Je n'aime pas (le dessin).   I don't like (art).

Je déteste (la physique).   I hate (physics).

La matière que j'aime le moins c'est ...
  The subject that I like least is ...

Getting to school

Comment vas-tu à l'école?
  How do you get to school?

J'y vais à pied.   I go (there) on foot.

J'y vais à vélo/en métro.
  I go (there) by bike/underground.

Je prends l'autobus.   I get the bus.

J'y vais par le train.   I go (there) by train.

Quand il pleut, je vais en voiture.
  When it rains, I go by car.

Your room

Dans ma chambre il y a un lit/bureau ...
  There's a bed/desk ... in my room.

Dans le salon il y a une table/télévision ...
  In the lounge there's a table/TV ...

la radio-cassette, la chaîne hi-fi, l'étagère
  tape recorder, hi-fi, shelf

Daily routine

Je me réveille.   I wake up.

Je me lève.   I get up.

Je me lave.   I wash myself.

Je m'habille.   I get dressed.

Je prends le petit déjeuner.   I eat breakfast.

Je quitte la maison.   I leave the house.

Je vais à l'école.   I go to school.

Health and fitness

Ça va?   How are you?

Je suis malade.   I'm ill.

J'ai mal à la tête.   I've got a headache.

J'ai mal à la gorge.   I've got a sore throat.

J'ai mal au ventre.   I've got a stomachache.

J'ai de la fièvre.   I've got a temperature.

Il faut aller chez le docteur.
  You must go to the doctor.

les bras, les mains, les pieds, les jambes
  arms, hands, feet, legs

Food and drink

Quel est ton plat préféré?
  What's your favourite meal?

Qu'est-ce que tu aimes manger?
  What do you like eating?

J'aime manger du/de la/de l'/des ...
  I like eating ...

Je mange du/de la/de l'/des ...   I eat ...

Je bois de l'eau.   I drink water.

de la viande, du beurre, du steak, du gâteau
  meat, butter, steak, cake

des haricots/tomates/pâtes, du poisson
  beans/tomatoes/pasta, fish

📺 Listening

When you're doing the listening activities in this book, don't watch the video at the same time – just listen! You won't have time to watch the people as they talk and complete each activity. So, first of all, find the clip you need for the activity and play it through once, just watching it. Then rewind the tape and prepare yourself to do the activity. Once you've done the activity, check your answer in the back, then sit back and watch the clip once more!

Listening out for single words

❗ REMEMBER Prepare yourself before listening. Choose a time when you won't be disturbed. Keep everything you need (pen, paper) next to you before you switch on the video.

Let's have a look at the pupils in the video and their favourite school subjects first: **Quelle est ta matière préférée?**

❓ What do you think – which subjects do you think the pupils like best? Make a list of them – in French, of course!

In a moment you're going to listen to the pupils and tick the subjects you hear them say. If you get a question like this in the exam, try and read the words on the exam paper before you listen and tick. So, have a look at these words and try to work out what they'll sound like on the video.

La biologie	**L'italien**	**Le dessin**
L'anglais	**Les sciences naturelles**	**Les sciences économiques**
La musique	**La gymnastique**	**Le français**
Les mathématiques	**Le sport**	**Les sciences physiques**

❗ REMEMBER This book uses the tu form for instructions (écoute/coche) – some exam boards use the **vous** form (écoutez/cochez) so don't be put off if you see those forms on the exam paper.

Now play the clip where the girl asks nine pupils: **Quelle est ta matière préférée?** and do the following activity.

◎ **Ecoute et coche les bons mots.** Listen and tick the words (above) that you hear.

In the next clip the girl asks four pupils: **Quelle est la matière que tu aimes le moins?** Listen to the answers and do the following activity.

◎ **Ecoute et fais une croix.** Listen and put a cross on the words (above) that you hear.

Could you recognise all the words as you had read them beforehand?

School subjects and transport

Now play the clip where Clémentine introduces her teachers and do the following activity.

◎ **Ecoute et fais correspondre les professeurs aux matières.** Listen and match the teachers to their subjects.

1 M. Casali	a le prof d'anglais
2 Miss Brown	b le prof de gymnastique
3 M. Royat	c le prof de français
4 M. Herbin	d le prof de sciences économiques
5 Mme Bertin	e le prof de mathématiques
6 Mlle Bonnet	f le prof d'italien

Find the clip where a female interviewer asks six women how they get to work: **Comment est-ce que vous allez à votre travail tous les jours?** Think for a moment about the sort of replies you might hear. Then do the activity.

◎ **Ecoute et fais correspondre les images aux six femmes.** Listen and match the pictures to the six women.

1 femme .... b..... et ....
2 femme ....
3 femme .... et ....
4 femme .... et ....
5 femme ...... et ...... et ......
6 femme ...... et ...... et ......

Did you notice how there were quite a lot of words in those answers that you didn't need? For example, one of the women talked about how she got to work when it was raining and when it was sunny – don't be distracted by this sort of detail, but just listen out for the words shown in the pictures.

🄷 If you look at the marks allotted to each question on the exam paper and you see that there are two marks for a task like the one above, you'll need to use that extra detail on the tape as well to get full marks.

Now play the clip where a woman asks six students how they get to school: **Comment allez-vous/vas-tu à l'école?** and do the following activity. Remember that it's only the words for the means of transport that you actually need here to get full marks – nothing else!

◎ **Ecoute et fais correspondre les images aux six étudiants.** Listen and match the pictures to the six students.

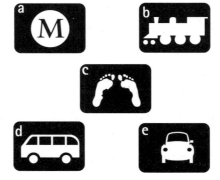

1 .... d ....
2 ....
3 ....
4 ....
5 ....
6 .... et ....

REMEMBER You can jot down the time code in the margin by each activity to help you rewind and fast forward the video.

REMEMBER If you don't catch one of the answers, just carry on and try the next speaker. Don't stop all together! On the next hearing, you can then fill in the one(s) you didn't hear first of all.

📺 Listening

Julien's room and daily routine

In the video, Julien shows you around his home – he uses some useful vocabulary for things you might have in your home.

(?) Look at the list below. Which of the things would you expect to find in the lounge (**le salon**) and which in Julien's room (**la chambre**)? Tick the list in pencil to prepare yourself for the video.

❗ REMEMBER BITESIZEfrench has its own revision team to help you if you run into problems while revising. The e-mail address is on the back of this book. 🔊

	le salon	la chambre de Julien
1 une télévision	☐	☐
2 un lit	☐	☐
3 un mobile	☐	☐
4 une chaise	☐	☐
5 une radio-cassette	☐	☐
6 un bureau	☐	☐
7 une étagère	☐	☐
8 une table	☐	☐
9 un stylo	☐	☐
10 une chaîne hi-fi	☐	☐
11 les photos	☐	☐

Now find the clip of Julien at home and do the following activity.

◎ **Ecoute et coche les bonnes cases.** Listen and tick the correct boxes. (above)

Next, Maxime tells you about his daily routine. Find the clip and play it once – watch Maxime carefully to see what he's doing each time he says something. What clues do you get from the video to help you understand what he's saying? You won't get visual clues like those in the exam, but you might hear some background noises or sound effects to help your understanding.

Now find the clip about Maxime's daily routine and do the following activity.

❗ REMEMBER In the exam you can only listen twice to the tape, but at this stage listen as many times as you need to.

◎ **Ecoute et remplis les blancs.** Listen and fill in the gaps.

Maxime **(a)** .... *à sept heures. Il se lève vers*
(b) .... *et puis il va directement à la*
(c) .... *Vers sept heures* **(d)** ....
il prend le **(e)** .... *Il mange des* **(f)** ....
et il boit du **(g)** .... *Vers* **(h)** ....
heures moins le quart il **(i)** .... *la maison.*

When you're filling in gaps in a text like this, don't worry if you can't get all the words written down immediately. Make notes for yourself on a piece of paper as you listen and then write the words in the gaps once the clip has finished. Listen as many times as you need to at this stage until all the gaps are full – how many times did you need to play the clip? Repeat the activity in a week's time and see if you can do it in fewer viewings!

Parts of the body

(?) How many parts of your body can you name – in French!? Have a go to prepare yourself for the next activity. Can you remember if they're **le** (masculine) words or **la** (feminine) words as well?

Find the start of the clip at the primary school where the little boy comes out of the cardboard box. Then do the following activity.

(◎) **Ecoute et range les mots.** Listen and put the words in the order you hear them.

f							

a *les bras*
b *les jambes*
c *le cou*
d *les pieds*
e *la poitrine*
f *la tête*
g *le ventre*
h *les mains*

(?) Do you know what all these words mean? Draw a little stick person in the box on the right and label it with the correct French words – it might help you remember them when you're in the exam!

(!) **REMEMBER** When you're putting words or pictures in order, just scribble a number by each one as you hear it – then fill the answer in neatly on the exam paper. You can then check your answer when you hear the recording a second time.

(13)

Practice activities

As you revise, it's a good idea to make notes for yourself, write down useful words and collect model texts or recordings to learn from. It's a good idea to have all these things together safely somewhere, so you can find them easily when you want to revise French. Get a file or a folder for yourself and label it **Ma révision française**. As you revise over the next few weeks, you can collect useful information in it and you can refer back to it for checking things or revising points again. Start your file off by writing a list of all your GCSE exam subjects – in French of course!

You heard quite a lot of 'food' words in this programme, so now would be a good time to gather some of them together to collect in your French revision file.

Start off by playing this first programme through and noting down any food or drink words you hear – don't stop the video at all as you listen. How many words did you pick out? Now you can listen in more detail to pick the words out. Choose a clip that has got a lot of food words in it, and this time concentrate really hard and see how many words you can pick out. You can listen to your chosen clip as often as you like. Write your words down on a piece of paper or record them on to cassette for future reference.

Speaking

Talking about your timetable

You're going to talk about your school subjects and what you do at school next. Look at the timetable below first of all and check you understand and can pronounce all the words on it.

REMEMBER Listen to the video if you're not sure how to pronounce some of the words – just copy the way the French people say things. You can listen as often as you like until you get it right!

EMPLOI DU TEMPS

	lundi	mardi	mercredi	jeudi	vendredi	samedi
1	maths	dessin	anglais	physique	français	informatique
2	sport	français	informatique	anglais	sport	maths
	Récréation	**Récréation**	**Récréation**	**Récréation**	**Récréation**	**Récréation**
3	maths	chimie	géographie	français	musique	histoire
	Pause	**Pause**	**Pause**	**Pause**	**Pause**	
4	biologie	informatique	physique	géographie	chimie	
5	français	histoire	–	maths	biologie	

Now you're going to give information about the timetable and say when you have certain lessons. Look at this example question first of all:

– *Quel est le troisième cours le mardi?*

Do you understand the question? You can look up a word you don't understand here in a dictionary or ask a friend what it means, but you can't do that when you're talking to the examiner in the actual exam. So if you're asked something you don't understand, just ask the examiner to repeat the question. Here's what you ask: **Comment?** (pardon?) or **Je n'ai pas compris** (I didn't understand) or **Pouvez-vous répéter la question, s'il vous plaît?** (Can you repeat the question, please?)

Now have a look at ways of answering the question. They're all correct, but each one makes the answer a bit longer – and that's a good habit to get into for the exam itself, where the more information you can give, the more marks you can score.

REMEMBER Always try to say as much as you can in your answers – every extra bit of information counts. And feel free to ask your own questions as well – just like you would in a normal conversation!

Exemple:
– Quel est le troisième cours le mardi?
– *Chimie.*
– *C'est la chimie.*
– *Le troisième cours le mardi, c'est la chimie.*
– *Le troisième cours le mardi, c'est la chimie. J'adore ça!*

◎ **Réponds aux questions.** Answer the questions. Try to give as much information as you can each time.

1 Quel est le deuxième cours le vendredi?
2 Quel est le premier cours le samedi?
3 Quel est le quatrième cours le lundi?
4 Quel est le cinquième cours le jeudi?
5 Quel est le troisième cours le mardi?

Telling the time

You'll probably come across times in your exam – maybe you'll need to say what time you get up in the morning, or you might hear some people talking about opening times of shops and museums on the tape. So, have a look at how you say the time in French:

A/C'est ...	*At/It's ...*
une heure	one o'clock
deux heures cinq	five past two
trois heures dix	ten past three
quatre heures et quart	quarter past four
cinq heures vingt	twenty past five
six heures vingt-cinq	twenty-five past six
sept heures et demie	half past seven
huit heures moins vingt-cinq	twenty-five to eight
neuf heures moins vingt	twenty to nine
dix heures moins le quart	quarter to ten
onze heures moins dix	ten to eleven
douze heures moins cinq	five to twelve
midi/minuit	midday/midnight

! **REMEMBER**
Whenever you look at your watch or a clock try and say the time in French. Check what you say against the list on this page to make sure you're getting it right!

Some questions you might come across about the time are:

Quelle heure est-il?	What's the time?
C'est ...	It's ...
A quelle heure ...?	What time ...?
A ...	At ...
Vers ...	About ...
Entre ... et ...	Between ... and ...

◎ **Quelle heure est-il?** What's the time? Look at these clocks and say each of the times out loud in French.

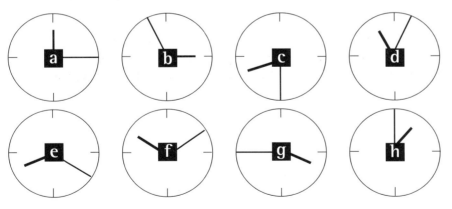

! **REMEMBER**
Try to sound as lively and as involved as possible when you speak.

◎ **Réponds aux questions.** Answer these questions.

1 *A quelle heure commencent les cours à l'école?*
2 *A quelle heure est-ce que tu te réveilles chaque matin?*
3 *A quelle heure fais-tu tes devoirs?*
4 *Tu quittes la maison à quelle heure le matin?*
5 *Tu prends le petit déjeuner à quelle heure?*

Speaking

Talking about what you eat

In the exam you may well get asked about what you eat or you might have to go shopping for food in a role play or explain how to make something, so it's important that you can name a few items of food and drink.

16

❗ REMEMBER You can add an opinion about the food you eat if you want to!

(?) Look at these sentence beginnings and check that you'd have something to say to finish them off in the exam. There are some ideas in the boxes, but you can use your own words as well.

Pour le petit déjeuner je mange … et je bois …

Pour le déjeuner je mange … et je bois …

bread and cheese and cola

Pour le dîner je mange … et je bois …

😊 croissant and hot chocolate

beans and steak

😝 fish and chips 😊

Practice questions

Can you answer these questions?

> *Quelle est ta matière préférée?*
> **Exemple:** *Ma matière préférée, c'est …*
> *Comment trouves tu le français?*
> **Exemple:** *Je le trouve …*
> *Tu te lèves à quelle heure?*
> **Exemple:** *Je me lève à …*
> *Comment vas-tu à l'école?*
> **Exemple:** *Je viens …/Je vais …*
> *Qu'est ce-que tu manges pour le petit déjeuner?*
> **Exemple:** *Je mange …*

🄷 *Décris une journée typique à l'école.*

See how much you can remember!

Can you…

- name eight school subjects?
- state four things you like about school?
- give four details about your daily routine, including times?
- name five items of food and four drinks?

Practice activity

Speaking French is easy to practise! You can say words out loud or in your head whenever you want to – just to get used to the sounds and feel comfortable with saying them. Next time you're walking to the shops, waiting for a bus or even having a bath, look around you – what can you see? Try and say some of the words in French – you can either say single words or try to make up a whole sentence or a question with them.

Exam focus: Giving your opinion

In nearly every topic area you cover, you'll have an opportunity to express your opinion on things. You might say what you think about music, people, places, fashions, food, school subjects, your hobbies ... the list really is endless. That means that there are a few phrases and words that you can learn and then use over and over again in different situations – so that's good news! Have a look at these four key phrases:

You might get symbols like these in the exam to show whether people like things or not, so this is what those phrases mean:

☺ 'I like ...'   ☺☺ 'I love ...'   ☹ 'I don't like'   ☹☹ 'I hate ...'

(?) Can you give your opinion on eight things, using the phrases above?

Exemple: – *J'aime l'école. Je déteste mes chaussures.*

The following way of giving an opinion is just as useful and even more impressive. You are basically using adjectives (describing words like 'fun', 'boring', 'easy') here to talk about things.

(?) Look at the words in the box and check you know what they all mean. Make a list of them to keep in your revision folder.

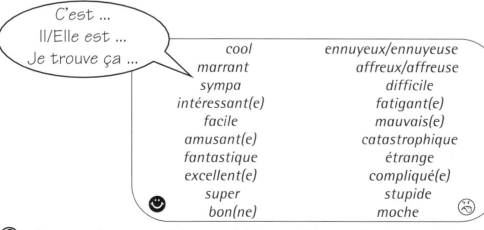

C'est ...
Il/Elle est ...
Je trouve ça ...

cool	*ennuyeux/ennuyeuse*
marrant	*affreux/affreuse*
sympa	*difficile*
intéressant(e)	*fatigant(e)*
facile	*mauvais(e)*
amusant(e)	*catastrophique*
fantastique	*étrange*
excellent(e)	*compliqué(e)*
super	*stupide*
bon(ne)	*moche*

(?) Can you give your opinion on eight more things, using the words in the box above to help you?

Exemple: *La musique classique, c'est ...*
Mon ami, il est ...
Ma sœur, elle est ...

REMEMBER
Giving an opinion really does liven up your writing or your speaking, so try and slip in a few opinions wherever you can!

REMEMBER
If you're talking about a male person, use **il est ...** with a masculine adjective (**bon/amusant**). If you're talking about a female person, use **elle est ...** with a feminine adjective (**bonne/ amusante**). However you can also say, **la musique,** (feminine word) **c'est bon** (masculine adjective) and **le sport,** (masculine word) **c'est bon** (masculine adjective), if you want to use **c'est ...**

Looking at single words

In the reading exam, you won't always have to read great long passages of French, you'll also have to read single words, for example on signs, posters or lists. The next two activities will help you focus on individual words.

(?) This next activity gives you a useful clue. Can you find it?

◎ **Cherche 12 choses à manger ou à boire.** Find 12 words for food and drink items in the grid.

```
T  A  B  R  F  P  O  M  M  E  C
H  T  I  P  O  U  L  E  T  H  R
E  I  S  S  A  Q  E  W  S  J  O
V  X  C  Z  O  E  U  F  O  H  I
F  H  U  P  A  I  N  K  U  L  S
P  O  I  S  S  O  N  T  P  C  S
V  W  T  M  K  G  R  U  E  A  A
D  C  H  O  C  O  L  A  T  F  N
J  A  M  B  O  N  T  Y  P  E  T
```

The clue was of course that the hidden words in the grid are all to do with food and drink items – don't miss clues like this in the exam!

There aren't any clues for this next activity, but can you find your own clues instead? How many of the words look like English words? **Côtelette**, for example, looks like 'cutlet', so there's a clue already! Try saying the words out loud too – that might help you recognise them.

◎ **Trouve l'intrus.** Find the odd word out in each list.

1 les maths	le sport	l'italien	les devoirs
2 le professeur	la salle de classe	la côtelette	l'emploi du temps
3 la gorge	la musique	les dents	la tête
4 bon	génial	affreux	formidable
5 la télévision	l'étagère	le lit	la maison
6 rouge	le dentifrice	blanc(he)	jaune
7 le train	les haricots	le croissant	les tartines

! REMEMBER Always try to learn nouns with their article **le** or **la**. Write word lists with the two types in different columns. You could start off with the words in the wordsearch!

! REMEMBER Try to read as much French as you can. You could ask your teacher if you can borrow some magazines or why not ask your penfriend to send you some of his/her old books and comics?

18

Reading short sentences and questions

In a reading activity, you might get six or seven short sentences to put in the correct order so they make sense. First of all, you need to read through the sentences to get an idea of what they are about.

(?) Look at these sentences. Can you tell what they are about?

a Je vais à l'école.
b Je me réveille.
c Je me lève.
d Je déjeune.
e Je fais mes devoirs.
f Je m'habille.
g Je prends le petit déjeuner.

◎ **Regarde les phrases encore une fois.** Look at the sentences again. Put them in the correct order to describe Marie's day from start to end.

> **! REMEMBER** A question like this is looking for the most likely sequence – just because you have breakfast in bed, doesn't mean everyone does!

You might also have to match sentence halves together or match questions to answers. Always match the ones you're really sure of first, then look at the ones that are left over. You don't always need to understand every word of the sentences to match them. For instance, if you see the question **Quelle est ta matière préférée?** and you recognise that **matière** means 'subject', then you can pick out an answer that has a school subject in it.

◎ **Fais correspondre.** Read the questions on the left and match them up with the answers on the right.

1 Quelle est ta matière préférée?	*a A pied.*
2 Comment est ton prof de français?	*b Oui, je l'aime beaucoup.*
3 Qu'est-ce que tu manges?	*c Le sport.*
4 A quelle heure vas-tu à l'école?	*d Du pain et de la confiture.*
5 Comment vas-tu à l'école?	*e A huit heures moins dix.*
6 Aimes-tu la musique classique?	*f Il est très sympa.*

`1c` ☐ ☐ ☐ ☐ ☐

> **! REMEMBER** In the exam, you won't get these helping instructions in English – you'll just get the French words, so make sure you always look at the French instructions carefully and can understand them before you do each activity.

Have a go at these sentence halves now – do the ones you're sure of first!

◎ **Fais correspondre.** Match up the sentence halves.

1 Je vais	*a en retard.*
2 Ma matière préférée,	*b parce qu'elle est sympa.*
3 J'aime le prof de sport,	*c de frites et de hamburgers.*
4 Je me réveille	*d c'est la musique.*
5 Je mange beaucoup	*e à l'école en voiture.*
6 Je suis souvent	*f à huit heures moins vingt.*

`1e` ☐ ☐ ☐ ☐ ☐

> **! REMEMBER** Write the answers in the correct place on the exam paper – you've got six boxes here, so each one needs to have a number and a letter in it.

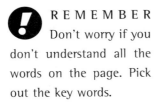
A matching activity

For some matching activities, you'll need to read longer pieces of text to find the answer. You might have to match signposts to people asking for places, or match pictures of sports to people talking about their hobbies. If there's quite a lot of text, it's important that you don't try to translate every word, as that will take you too long. First of all, scan through all the texts to get an idea as to what the activity is about. Have a go with this example:

(?) Read the texts to get an idea about the activity..

REMEMBER
Don't worry if you don't understand all the words on the page. Pick out the key words.

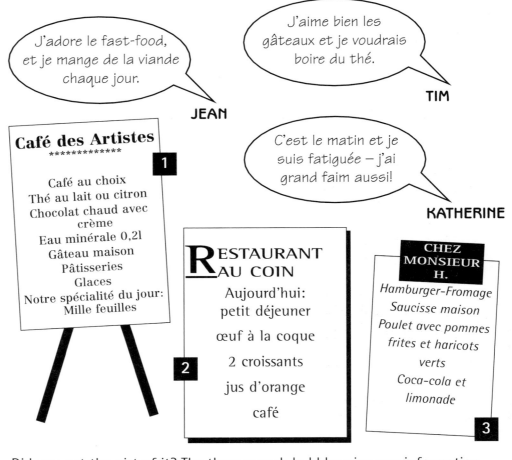

Did you get the gist of it? The three speech bubbles give you information about three people's eating needs and the menus below give you the types of food available. So, the task? Well, you choose a menu for each of the people. Let's find a menu for Jean together – look at his speech bubble. He likes fast food and meat in particular so look at the items on the three menus and find one that has got hamburgers or hot dogs, for example.

REMEMBER
Match the speech bubbles and menus that you're sure of first – you don't have to find Jean's menu first just because that's the first speech bubble you see.

(◎) **Fais correspondre les bulles aux cartes.** Match the speech bubbles to the menus.

Jean ☐   *Tim* ☐   *Katherine* ☐

Re-ordering a dialogue

📺 Do you remember why Clémentine was feeling ill in the video? Below is the transcript of her conversation with her mother and the pharmacist – but it's in the wrong order! After you've done the activity, you can check your answer against the video or in the back of this book.

When you're putting a dialogue in the correct order, use your common sense: it's unlikely that a question will follow another question and the same person won't speak directly after themselves!

Chez Clémentine

a Clémentine: Non, j'ai mal à la gorge.
b Clémentine: Pâle? Ma mère trouvait que je suis pâle. J'ai un peu mal à la gorge. Peut-être que je suis malade.
c Mère: Mais oui? Tu es un peu pâle.
d Clémentine: Oui?
e Mère: Ça va?
f Mère: Clémentine?

| f | | | | |

A la pharmacie

a Pharmacien: Non, je ne crois pas. Tu as vu le docteur?
b Pharmacien: Ah, alors, ce n'est pas un rhume. Tu as de la fièvre?
c Pharmacien: C'est pour toi? Tu as d'autres symptômes? Mal à la tête?
d Clémentine: Quelque chose pour le mal de gorge.
e Pharmacien: Bonjour, Clémentine. Qu'est-ce que tu désires?
f Clémentine: Non.
g Clémentine: Bonjour.
h Clémentine: Non.
i Clémentine: Je ne sais pas.

| g | | | | | | |

> **! REMEMBER**
> When you're putting a dialogue into the correct order, look for the opening speech first – it'll probably be a greeting.

Practice activity

Look at the phrases on page 9 and choose one section that you'd like to learn today. Start off by reading the French and the English words – say them out loud or in your head.

Then cut out some pieces of paper – you'll need one piece for each phrase. Copy a French phrase on to each piece of paper, then close this book.

Go through the pieces of paper one at a time and write the English meaning on the back of each piece in pencil.

Then open this book again and check what you've written. If you've written the correct meaning already, then copy over it in pen. If the meaning is wrong, then rub it out. Go through all your pieces of paper in this way.

Repeat the process – writing meanings in pencil and then checking them and saying them to yourself – until all your pieces of paper have got both French and English words written in pen.

You've now got a handy set of vocabulary cards – shuffle them up and look at one side again tomorrow. Can you say what's on the other side?

Writing

Spelling words

You need to impress the examiner that your French spelling is accurate. Test yourself on this first activity about school subjects.

◎ **Retrouve et écris les mots.** Work out and write down the words.

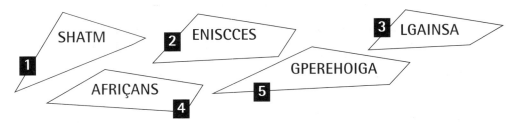

SHATM **1**

2 ENISCCES

3 LGAINSA

GPEREHOIGA **5**

AFRIÇANS **4**

⊘ What other subjects do you do at school? Write them down.

What do you do if there's a word you want to write in French but you don't know what it is? For example, you might need to write the word 'potatoes' on a shopping list, but you just can't think of the French word for 'potatoes'. Do you a) ask a friend? b) ask your teacher when you're next at school? c) look it up in a dictionary? d) think of something else to write? Well, all these are good ways of finding out more French words, but in the exam you certainly won't be able to do a) or b), and c) might take you too long for every word. So maybe you need to start thinking about d). Just because the exam paper says 'chop', for example, it doesn't mean that an answer like **viande** (meat) or **du porc** (pork) won't get you any marks. Always try to write something on the exam paper – a blank answer will never get you any marks, but a near miss might score you some points! So, have a go at the next activity without using a dictionary or asking anybody – how do you cope?

◎ **Ecris la liste.** Write the list.

1 Chop:	———————————
2 Potatoes:	———————————
3 Butter:	———————————
4 Bread:	———————————
5 Water:	———————————
6 Apples:	———————————
7 Wine:	———————————
8 Sugar:	———————————

Have you got any blank spaces on your list? Can you really not think of anything to write? Look at the answers at the back of the book and write the words on the list. Make sure you learn those words!

❗ **REMEMBER** Try to check your written answers in a dictionary or in the answer section at the back of this book – then you'll get your spellings correct.

❗ **REMEMBER** Draft notes in rough first. Try to give as much information as you can in your answer.

Adapting a model text

Even in the writing exam, you'll probably have to do some reading as well. In the next activity, you're given a model text and then you have to write a similar one yourself. Don't ignore a model like this when you get one – even if you can't understand it all, there'll be some useful language in it for you to recycle.

(?) How much do you understand in this text? Which words or phrases do you think might be useful for writing your own text? Underline them.

> Je m'appelle Henri et j'habite Annecy. Je me lève à huit heures et quart. Je mange un œuf pour le petit-déjeuner. Je bois une tasse de thé. Je prends l'autobus pour aller à l'école. Ma matière préférée, c'est l'histoire. Je n'aime pas l'anglais.

Look at this underlined text (the right way up!) and compare it with your underlining. Are they the same?

> (upside-down text) Je m'appelle Henri et j'habite Annecy. Je me lève à huit heures et quart. Je mange un œuf pour le petit-déjeuner. Je bois une tasse de thé. Je prends l'autobus pour aller à l'école. Ma matière préférée, c'est l'histoire. Je n'aime pas l'anglais.

Now you can write your own text like the one you've just read. The following is just a practice test to get you started – in the exam you'll be more likely to have to write about yourself.

(◎) **Ecris un texte avec ces détails.** Write a text with these details.

> My name's Andy.
> I live in Leeds. I get up at half past eight. I eat a croissant for breakfast. I drink a cup of coffee. I go to school by bike. My favourite subject is chemistry. I don't like French.

Check your piece of writing against the answer at the back of the book. Correct any mistakes and highlight the phrases you underlined above. Keep your text in your revision folder or file so that you can revise from it again later on to check that you remember everything!

(b) *Ecris une lettre à ton correspondant. Décris:*
- *ta journée à l'école*
- *quand tu te lèves*
- *ton déjeuner*
- *ton voyage à l'école*
- *ta matière préférée.*

(!) REMEMBER When you do a written task like this one, tick off each item as you write about it – then you won't miss anything out!

Writing

Writing about transport

You can practise writing a few simple sentences now! The graph on the right shows the results of a survey that asked: **Comment allez-vous à votre travail?**

REMEMBER
If you've got an example answer, then follow its pattern for your answers.

◎ **Ecris les phrases.** Write sentences.

Exemple:
Dix personnes vont à pied.

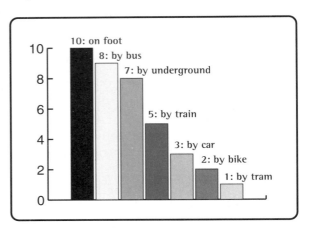

Practice questions

Can you answer these questions – in writing?

Quelle est ta matière préférée?

Quelles matières n'aimes-tu pas?

Qu'est-ce que tu aimes manger?

A quelle heure fais-tu tes devoirs?

Comment vas-tu à l'école?

Comment tes profs vont-ils à l'école?

h *Qu'est-ce que tu fais chaque journée?*

Practice activity

Check to see how much you know!

Can you...

- write down eight school subjects?
- write down six items of food?
- write down five things to drink?
- write down three things you do every day?
- write down four forms of transport?

GrammarZONE

📺 You will have noticed lots of examples in the video of the two words for 'a' and 'the' in French. **Le** and **la** mean 'the' – **un** and **une** mean 'a'. **Le** and **un** words are 'masculine' – (m) for short – and **la** and **une** words are 'feminine' – (f) for short. If you're not sure whether a French word is masculine or feminine, you can look it up in a dictionary:

vélo (m)	⇨	masculine	⇨	*le/un vélo*
voiture (f)	⇨	feminine	⇨	*la/une voiture*

If a noun begins with a vowel (a, e, i, o, u) or an 'h', then you use **l'** for 'the'.

autobus (m)	⇨	masculine	⇨	*l'autobus/un autobus*
église (f)	⇨	feminine	⇨	*l'église/une église*
homme (m)	⇨	masculine	⇨	*l'homme/un homme*

◎ Copy these words into lists – one for **le/l'** and **un** (masculine) words and one for **la/l'** and **une** (feminine) words. You can use a dictionary if you're not sure.

café   viande   professeur   beurre   école   tartine

If you're using plural nouns ('book<u>s</u>', 'girl<u>s</u>', 'present<u>s</u>') then you use **les** for 'the'.

homme (m)	⇨	masculine plural	⇨	*les hommes*
fille (f)	⇨	feminine plural	⇨	*les filles*

Most French plurals are like English – you just add an 's' on the end: **école/écoles**. Like with most rules, there are some exceptions, such as **hôpital/hôpitaux** and **château/châteaux**.

📺 Did you notice in the video how the people talked about different foods? Look at these sentences – what do you notice about the word for 'some'?

Je bois du café.   Je mange de la viande.   J'achète de l'eau.   J'ai des tartines.

That's right – in French, you use **du, de la, de l'** and **des** for 'some'. In English, we often leave it out altogether:

Je bois du café.   I drink coffee.
J'achète de l'eau.   I'm buying some water.

◎ Match up the French words for 'the' with their equivalent for 'some'.

le	*des*
la	*de l'*
l'	*du*
les	*de la*

◎ Fill in the gaps with **du, de la, de l'** or **des**.

1 Je mange .... poisson.
2 Je voudrais .... frites, s'il vous plaît.
3 Je bois .... chocolat chaud.
4 J'achète .... limonade.
5 Vous voulez .... biscottes?

Personal Life

This section is about

- Family and friends

- Interests and hobbies

- Special occasions

- Holidays

- Pocket money

This section is all about your personal life and that includes your character and appearance, your family and pets, your hobbies and free time activities and how much pocket money you get. These are all topics that you'll need to know about for your exam.

Tu as des frères ou des sœurs? Have you got any brothers and sisters? **Il/elle a quel âge?** How old is he/she? In this section you'll meet a number of French teenagers who talk about their family (**la famille**) and who describe themselves and their brothers and sisters.

Où habites-tu? Where do you live? **Quelle est la date de ton anniversaire?** When's your birthday? **Tes parents sont comment?** What are your parents like? In the exam, the examiner is bound to get personal and he/she will want to know lots about you – so be prepared beforehand! Make sure you've got a good stock of phrases ready to bring out as soon as the examiner starts quizzing you about yourself! But don't worry if you're not sure yet, as once you've worked through the activities in this section, you should be able to describe yourself and your family – and that's something that you almost certainly will be asked to do in the exam!

Hobbies and sports are another favourite exam topic – **Es-tu sportif/sportive?** What sort of

sports do you do and which sports can't you stand? Make sure you know plenty of French words for sports and free-time activities – just watching the video a few times should give you plenty of ideas. Do you like group sports (**les sports collectifs**) or team sports (**les sports d'équipe**)? Or do you find sport too tiring (**fatigant**) altogether?

And what about celebrations through the year? Do you get lots of presents (**cadeaux**) for your birthday? And does everybody say 'Happy Birthday' – **Bon anniversaire!**? You'll find out how to give the date of your birthday in this section – and once you know how to do that, you'll be able to give the date for lots of other events and activities during the year too.

Do you dream about visiting South America (**l'Amérique du Sud**) or Russia (**la Russie**)? Well, in this section you'll find out where some French teenagers want to go. Which country would you like to visit – **Quel pays voudrais-tu visiter?**

Finally in this section, you'll find out how much pocket money some teenagers get and what sort of part-time jobs they do – and that's a topic that's sure to interest you!

So let's get started – **allons-y!**

⊙ These phrases will be really useful for your exam, so see if you can try and learn them!

Family and friends

Est-ce que tu as des frères ou des sœurs?
    Have you got any brothers and sisters?

J'ai un frère et deux sœurs.
    I've got one brother and two sisters.

Non, je suis enfant unique.
    No, I'm an only child.

Mon frère/il s'appelle ...
    My brother/he is called ...

Ma sœur/elle s'appelle ...
    My sister/she is called ...

Il/elle a ... ans.   He/she is ... years old.

J'ai un chien/un chat.   I've got a dog/cat.

Mon père/ma mère travaille à ...
    My father/mother works at ...

Il/elle est mignon(ne)/timide/sympa ...
    He/she is sweet/shy/nice ...

*Il/elle a des cheveux bruns/noirs/raides/
    longs.*   He/she has got brown/black/
    straight/long hair.

Il/elle a des yeux bleus/verts/marron.
    He/she has got blue/green/brown eyes.

Il/elle porte des lunettes.
    He/she wears glasses.

Interests and hobbies

Qu'est-ce que tu aimes faire?
    What do you like doing?

Est-ce que tu aimes danser/nager/lire?
    Do you like dancing/swimming/reading?

J'aime faire du sport/écouter de la musique ...
    I like doing sport/listening to music ...

J'adore regarder la télé/aller au cinéma ...
    I love watching TV/going to the
    cinema ...

Quels sports fais-tu?
    What sports do you do?

Je joue au football/tennis/basketball ...
    I play football/tennis/basketball ...

Je fais du ski/du vélo/du bowling ...
    I ski/cycle/go bowling ...

Special occasions

Quelle est la date de ton anniversaire?
    When's your birthday?

C'est le quatorze janvier.   It's January 14.

février, mars, avril, mai
    February, March, April, May

juin, juillet, août, septembre
    June, July, August, September

octobre, novembre, décembre
    October, November, December

Holidays

Quel pays voudrais-tu visiter?
    Which country would you like to visit?

J'aimerais bien visiter ...   I'd like to visit ...

Je vais en France/Italie/Angleterre/Espagne.
    I'm going to France/Italy/England/Spain.

Je suis allé(e) ...   I went ...

Je vais aller ...   I'm going to go ...

Pocket money

Tu reçois combien d'argent de poche?
    How much pocket money do you get?

*Qu'est-ce que tu achètes avec ton argent de
    poche?*   What do you buy with your
    pocket money?

Est-ce que tu travailles le week-end?
    Do you work at the weekend?

Je gagne l'argent en gardant les enfants.
    I earn money by looking after children.

Je travaille dans un magasin/un restaurant.
    I work in a shop/restaurant.

27

Personal Life

⊙ Listening

Listening to lots of short answers

In the video, nine teenagers are asked if they've got any brothers and sisters: **Tu as des frères ou des sœurs?** In the exam you might also hear several people giving information about themselves, their family, their school etc. That means that you're going to hear quite a few voices and a lot of information, so it's important that you're prepared before the tape starts. The first thing to do, is to look at the task itself, so you know what you've got to listen out for. So, have a look at the following task.

◎ **Ecoute et note les réponses.** Listen and note the answers.

Tu as des frères ou des sœurs?

1 ...... d ....
2 ....
3 ....
4 ....
5 ....
6 ....
7 ....
8 .... et ....
9 ....

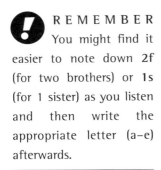

Now check that:
- you understand the instruction
- you understand what the pictures mean
- you know where you've got to write the answer
- you know what sort of an answer you've got to write (i.e. the letter – a, b, c, d or e – corresponding to the correct picture)
- you've got a pen or pencil ready to note down the answer.

Now find the clip on the video where the nine teenagers reply to the survey **(enquête)** about the number of brothers and sisters they've got, and do the activity above.

Have a go at a similar activity now to see how well you can pick out details! Find the clip where eight people are giving the ages of their brothers and sisters and do this activity.

◎ **Ecoute et note les âges.** Listen and note the ages.

Les frères	Les sœurs
1 ...... 5	5 ....
2 .... et	6 ....
3 .... et	7 ....
4	8 ....

28

REMEMBER You might find it easier to note down 2f (for two brothers) or 1s (for 1 sister) as you listen and then write the appropriate letter (a–e) afterwards.

REMEMBER As you're not in the exam now, you can listen to the video again and again until you've got all the answers! You can also pause the video when you like to give yourself more time.

Listening for detail

Clémentine introduces her family on the video, and she gives lots of useful information about them.

(?) What sort of things do you need to say to introduce your family? Can you say four sentences to describe your family – in French, of course!

Thinking of ideas yourself before you listen to the tape is a good idea as you might then recognise some key words. For instance, if Clémentine is going to introduce her family, you can expect to hear words like **mère, père** and **frère** and maybe she'll use verbs like **travaille, habite** and **aime**. Do you know what those words mean?

Now find the clip where Clémentine is talking about her family and do the next activity.

(◎) **Ecoute et remplis les formulaires en français.** Listen and fill in the forms in French.

Mère – nom:	[1]
Age:	[1]
Travail:	[1]
Adore:	[1]
Caractère:	[1]

Frère – nom:	[1]
Age:	[1]
Caractère:	[1]
Adore:	[1]
Aime le plus (animaux):	[1]
A combien?:	[1]

Père – travail:	[1]
Passe-temps (2 choses):	[2]
Caractère:	[1]

(h) *Ecoute encore une fois et réponds aux questions en français.*

1 La mère de Clémentine, elle travaille où?
2 Quel âge a-t-elle?
3 Qu'est-ce qu'elle boit comme une snob?
4 Qui est Emile?
5 Qu'est-ce qu'il a dans sa chambre?
6 Qui sont les meilleurs amis d'Emile?
7 Qui travaille à la poste?
8 A quelle heure va-t-il au travail?
9 Avec qui va le père de Clémentine au café?
10 Est-ce que Clémentine aime beaucoup son père?

REMEMBER You can make notes for yourself in rough or pencil as you listen and you can then fill in the forms neatly afterwards.

REMEMBER The numbers in brackets – [1] [2] – show how many marks are available. To get two marks when there's a [2], you'll need to write down two details.

REMEMBER When you get questions like these in the listening exam, you don't have to answer in full sentences – single words or short phrases will do.

 # Listening

Listening for specific words

Isabelle is asking people about sports they can do. What sports do you know in French already? Lots of sports look and sound similar to the English words, so that's a great help when you're listening to people talking in French! You should easily be able to recognise words like **football, base-ball** and **hockey**.

(?) Look at the sports in the box below and see how many of them you know. Can you pronounce them out loud or in your head?

> *On fait ... du ski.*
> *du hockey sur glace.*
> *du patin à roulettes.*
>
> *On joue ... au base-ball.*
> *au foot.*
> *au rugby.*
>
> *On fait ...*
> *de l'escalade.*
> *du bateau.*
> *du vélo.*
> *de la natation.*
> *de la planche à voile.*
> *du deltaplane.*

Now watch the clip of some of those sports and practise saying the words as you see each one on the screen.

Let's do a practice activity with sports now. Find the clip on the video where seven teenagers are asked about the sports that they do: **Tu fais du sport?** Then look at the following activity and run through the names for the sports depicted.

(◎) **Ecoute et remplis la grille.** Listen and complete the grid.

	a	b	c	d	e	f	g	h
1 MARIE								
2 BERTRAND								
3 PHILIPPE								
4 ALEXANDRE								
5 PATRICIA								
6 NICOLAS								
7 SABRINA								

! R E M E M B E R
You can always listen to the video to check your pronunciation of French words.

! R E M E M B E R
In the exam, you'll hear **un, deux** etc. before each person speaks in an activity like this, so you'll know which person you're listening to each time.

30

Listening to dates

Dates often come up in questions, and in the video several people give the date of their birthday – listening to this clip is good practice for dates. First of all, let's check you know the months and numbers in French. You can check the months on page 27 and if you want further details on actual dates have a look at page 34.

(?) Can you say these dates in French?

Find the clip where eight children reply to the question: **Quelle est la date de ton anniversaire?** and do the following activity.

◎ **Ecoute et écris les bonnes dates.** Listen and write the correct dates.

1 ... le 23 avril ....
2 ....
3 ....
4 ....
5 ....
6 ....
7 ....
8 ....

For a final listening activity here find the clip where four people reply to the question: **Quel pays voudrais-tu visiter?** Do the following activities.

(?) Make a list of all the countries you know in French first of all.

◎ **Ecoute et écris les pays mentionnés.** Listen and write down the countries mentioned.

1 ALEXANDRE ... l'Allemagne ......   *3 SABRINA ....*
2 ALICE ....   *4 CONSTANCE ....*

REMEMBER
If you have to write dates – in a letter or text, for example – you can write **le** 12/04 instead of writing it out in full. Remember the first number is the day (12 = twelfth) and the second is the month (4 = april).

REMEMBER
If you've spent time learning vocabulary, you'll be able to recognise more words on the tape in the listening exam!

Practice activity

You'll need your remote control for this activity, as you're going to pause and rewind the video quite a lot so that you can practise your French pronunciation!

Choose a short clip from this programme that you like and play it through once. Check that you've got the gist of the conversation and you know what it's about. After you've played it through once, jot down five key words or phrases from it and say them out loud. Then play the video again – this time you're going to pause after each sentence and repeat it after the speaker.

So, play a sentence, pause the video, say the words yourself, rewind the video and listen again to check your pronunciation and intonation. Carry on doing this until you're happy with the way you sound!

● ● ● Speaking

Talking about yourself

In the speaking exam, the examiner will almost certainly want to know a few things about you. He or she will probably ask you a few general questions about youself to start the exam off, so make sure you go in with ready answers – you can work them out on this page.

32

! REMEMBER It's important that you learn the names for the letters of the French alphabet as you may need to spell words and names in the exam.

◎ **Réponds aux questions.** Answer the questions.
Use your own name and then use those on the right for extra practice.

Exemple:
– Comment t'appelles-tu?
– Je m'appelle *Oliver.*
– Et ton nom de famille?
– *Powell.*
– Comment ça s'écrit?
– *P-O-W-E-L-L.*

Dominique Legrand
Pascal Dubois
Juliette Leconte
Simone Lartigue

In the exam, you won't always be asked about yourself. You might have to take on the role of a French teenager and give information about him or her. To do this, you'll be give a role play card with words or picture cues on. That's what you can practise in this next activity.

◎ **Réponds aux questions.** Answer the questions.
The personal details are all on the right, so use them for your answers.

Exemple:
– Quelle est la date de ton anniversaire?
– C'est *le douze janvier.*
– Quel âge as-tu?
– J'ai *seize* ans.
– Est-ce que tu as des frères ou des sœurs?
– Oui, j'ai *un frère.* Il s'appelle *Marc.*
– Combien d'argent de poche reçois-tu?
– Je reçois *dix livres chaque mois.*
– Qu'est-ce que tu fais dans ton temps libre?
– Je *fais de l'escalade et j'écoute de la musique.*

- birthday – 16 June
- 17 years old
- sister (Roz), brother (Steve)
- £2 per week
- hobbies: playing computer games and swimming

! REMEMBER Ask your teacher when you're not sure how a word or phrase is pronounced. You can then practise the pronunciation (with a tape recorder) before you use the word or phrase.

The six questions below are very important if you want to find out information about people – see if you can learn them and make sure you've got a ready reply for each one by the time of your exam.

Comment t'appelles tu?

Où habites-tu?

Quel âge as-tu?

C'est quand ton anniversaire?

Tu as des frères ou des sœurs?

Qu'est ce que tu fais le week-end?

Making your answers more detailed

📺 In the video, did you notice the different ways of answering a question? There's usually more than one way of doing it. For example, if someone asks you, 'What are you doing at the weekend?' you could reply, a) 'Nothing much', b) I'm going to the cinema', c) I'm meeting my friends on Saturday and we're going to go shopping. I can't wait!' Which answer do you think is more interesting? Well, it has to be c) because it contains the most information and an opinion. Get in the habit of answering questions with as much detail as possible – and you can give your opinion on every topic!

Let's look at a question now: *Quel est ton passe-temps préféré?* And the answers? Well, look at these key phrases:

> *J'adore ... (+ infinitive of a verb such as nager, danser, lire)*
> *Mon sport préféré, c'est ...*
> *Je m'entraîne ...*
> *J'aime ... parce que ...*
> *On a ... heures de sport à l'école par semaine.*

❓ **Quel est ton passe-temps préféré?** Answer the question with as much detail as possible. The phrases above will help you.

When you're given questions in the exam, you're being given a big help! If you're careful, you can use the question to help you with your answer. How? Well, you just repeat part of the question to make your answer sound more impressive. So, let's look at a question:

> *Qu'est-ce que tu fais le week-end?*

Do you know how to answer that? Well, you could just say **la télévision** but that's very short. Why not try to make your answer longer by using some of the words from the question? For example, you could say, **Le week-end, je regarde la télé.** You could even go on to give more details, **J'aime surtout les émissions de sport.**

◎ **Réponds aux questions.** Answer the questions. Use some of the ideas in the boxes to help you.

Exemple: – Qu'est-ce que tu fais ce soir?
         – *Je vais au cinéma avec mon ami. On va voir un film d'aventure. Ça va être formidable!*

| do my homework – boring! | stay at home – eat good food | visit my sister – like her a lot | play squash – very tiring | listen to music – favourite band is ... | meet friends in town – go to the shops |

🅗 *Qu'est-ce que tu aimes faire le week-end?* See if you can say seven sentences to describe what you enjoy doing at the weekend. Give your opinion and as much detail as possible.

Personal Life

> **REMEMBER**
> Speak clearly and slowly – there's no need to rush!

> **REMEMBER**
> Using words like **et, mais, puis** and **parce que** will help to keep your speech flowing.

> **REMEMBER**
> Keep a list of key phrases in your revision folder to use in the future.

Speaking

REMEMBER If you need some extra support with your revision, you can contact the BITESIZE team via the internet. The e-mail address is on the back of this book. ✆

Talking about days, months and seasons

You can easily add detail to most things you say just by adding a time, a date or a time of the year. You'll find the months of the year on page 27, so they're worth learning for a start. Do you know the following 'time' words?

Demain ...	*Aujourd'hui ...*	*Hier ...*
Le premier avril ...	*Le deux juillet*	*L'année passée ...*
Le trois mars ...	*Le quatre octobre ...*	*L'année prochaine ...*
Lundi matin ...	*L'après-midi ...*	*Après ...*
En été/en hiver ...	*Chaque jour ...*	*Avant ...*
Le week-end	*Ce soir ...*	*Bientôt ...*

◎ **Dis les phrases.** Say sentences using the words above. Check your sentences with your teacher or French assistant!

Exemple: – L'anniversaire de mon frère, c'est le deux juillet.
               – Hier je suis allé(e) en ville.

Practice questions

Can you answer these questions?

Comment t'appelles-tu?
Exemple: *Je m'appelle ...*
Où habites-tu?
Exemple: *J'habite ...*
Quel âge as-tu?
Exemple: *J'ai ... ans.*
Est-ce que tu as des frères/sœurs?
Exemple: *Oui/non ...*
Quelle est la date de ton anniversaire?
Exemple: *C'est le ...*
Quels sports fais-tu?
Exemple: *Je fais/joue ...*

h *Décris ta famille.*

See how much you can remember!

Can you...

■   say the months of the year?

■   count to 31?

■   describe four people (family or friends)?

■   name five sports?

■   name three hobbies?

■   name four 'time' phrases or words?

Practice activity

Find a friend from your French class or a member of your family who speaks French and spend a few minutes working on the practice questions above. The other person asks you the questions and you give an answer – just like you will in the exam. Try to give as full an answer as you can with lots of details. You can do this with all the 'Practice questions' sections in this book – remember to practise asking the questions too!

📺 Did you notice in the video, that some sentences used an 'infinitive'? An infinitive is just the verb like **aller** (to go), **faire** (to do) and **jouer** (to play). What verbs do you know in French?

Using a phrase with an infinitive is easy. Look at these examples:

J'aime **jouer** *au football.*	⇨	I like playing football.
Je veux **visiter** *Paris.*	⇨	I want to visit Paris.
Je vais **aller** *en France.*	⇨	I'm going to go to France.

◎ Fill in the gaps with the infinitive in brackets.

1 J'adore [eat] .... *du chocolat.*
2 Je vais [do] .... *mes devoirs.*
3 On veut [go to] .... *au théâtre demain.*
4 Ils aiment [dance] ....
5 J'aime [read] .... *les magazines.*

Have a look at number 4 and 5 above. What do you notice about the verb **aimer**? Yes, it's got different endings. Look at these examples of different endings:

Ils adorent leur père.   Nous aimons aller au café.   Aimez-vous le français?

It's just the same in English: 'I go' and 'he g**oes**'. Lots of French verbs follow the same pattern for their endings and the biggest group follows the pattern of **jouer**. Let's have a look at it:

jouer – to play	écouter – to listen	habiter – to live
je joue	*j'écoute*	*j'habite*
*tu joue***s**	*tu*	*tu* ....
il/elle/on joue	*il/elle/on*	*il/elle/on* ....
*nous jou***ons**	*nous*	*nous* ....
*vous jou***ez**	*vous*	*vous* ....
*ils/elles jou***ent**	*ils/elles*	*ils/elles* ....

◎ Can you fill in the gaps for *écouter* and *habiter* (above)?

📺 Did you notice people in the video talking about their brothers and sisters?

Est-ce que tu **as** *des frères ou des sœurs?   Oui, j'*ai *deux frères.*

The verb **avoir** (to have) doesn't follow the pattern of **jouer** and nor does **être** (to be). These are two important verbs that you'll use a lot. Have a look at them and see if you can learn them.

avoir – to have	être – to be
*j'***ai**	*je* **suis**
tu **as**	*tu* **es**
il/elle/on **a**	*il/elle/on* **est**
nous **avons**	*nous* **sommes**
vous **avez**	*vous* **êtes**
ils/elles **ont**	*ils/elles* **sont**

Reading

Widening your vocabulary

You'll find the reading exam a lot easier, if you know a lot of French words before you go in – that's why it's important to learn French vocabulary regularly. This page starts you off with some key words from this section, but it's also up to you to look back over your classroom work and find key words and phrases to learn.

◎ **Trouve sept mots.** Find seven words.

ONCLESAMERETWRSEAREFRERESAWSŒURSDPERETANTEASCOUSIN(E)

If you're going to write those seven family words down to learn, try to write down their gender as well (**le, la**) – it's a good habit to get into.

Now let's look at some words for hobbies.

◎ **Fais correspondre les phrases avec les passe-temps.** Match the sentences to the hobbies.

1 Il y a onze joueurs dans une équipe. On y joue à Elland Road et Old Trafford par exemple.

2 C'est un passe-temps très actif! On écoute de la musique. On le fait souvent à la disco.

3 On regarde beaucoup de films.

4 C'est un passe-temps très paresseux – on est dans le salon ou dans sa chambre et on regarde un écran.

5 Pour ce passe-temps il faut aller peut-être à la bibliothèque.

a lire

b jouer au football

c regarder la télé

d danser

e aller au cinéma

And finally here are four holiday destinations that you might need to know about in the exam. (You'll find more countries on page 84.)

◎ **Ecris les mots.** Write the words.

1 ALEITI   *2* EGPNASE

3 GAAELEMLN   *4* FNECRA

36

REMEMBER Make sure that you revise from the classroom work you've done over the past few years as well as this book – your teacher will help you if you're not sure exactly what you need to learn.

REMEMBER Collect all your useful French vocabulary together safely – don't just do the activity and then forget about the words straight away.

True/false statements

In the exam you'll find different types of reading activities. You might have to answer questions in French or English, do multiple-choice exercises, work out which sentences are true or false and maybe match pictures to words as well. So make sure that you read the instructions carefully for each activity and not just the text that goes with it! The next two activities are typical true/false tasks – you'll probably get one of these in your exam.

◎ **Regarde la photo. Vrai, faux ou je ne sais pas?** Look at the photo. True, false or I don't know?

	vrai	faux	je ne sais pas
1 La fille porte des lunettes.	☐	☐	☐
2 Elle a des cheveux assez courts.	☐	☐	☐
3 Elle porte un chapeau.	☐	☐	☐
4 Elle a trente ans.	☐	☐	☐
5 Elle a des cheveux marron.	☐	☐	☐

h This next task requires a bit more reading from you. First of all read through the text to get the gist of it.

> Beaucoup de jeunes habitent encore chez la mère ou le père. Et ce sont les jeunes hommes qui adorent habiter chez les parents. Mais pourquoi aiment-ils y habiter? Parce que: «C'est confortable chez maman.» Il y a beaucoup de fils qui ne veulent pas faire la cuisine ou repasser leurs vêtements. Les garçons restent alors à la maison. Et les filles? Qu'est-ce qu'elles font? Elles louent un appartement et rendent visite à leurs parents quand elles veulent.

Now look at the true/false statements below and work your way through them one by one. You'll need to keep going back to the text to find the answers. If you get stuck on one statement, don't stop altogether, just go on to the next one and see if you can answer it.

h *Lis l'article. Les phrases sont-elles vraies ou fausses?*

	vrai	faux
1 Les jeunes n'habitent jamais chez les parents.	☐	☐
2 Plus de garçons que de filles restent à la maison.	☐	☐
3 La maison des parents est souvent affreuse.	☐	☐
4 Beaucoup de garçons n'aiment pas faire la cuisine.	☐	☐
5 Les filles habitent souvent un appartement.	☐	☐
6 Les filles ne rendent jamais visite à leurs parents.	☐	☐

! REMEMBER The French word **vrai(es)** means 'correct' and **faux/fausses** means 'false' so make sure that you tick the box you intend to each time.

How did you do? Did you manage to tick true or false for all of those statements? If not, check the answers at the back of the book and see if you can find the answer in the text now.

 # Reading

Picking out key information

Jack's French exchange partner has sent him a leaflet of all the things there are to do in his town. You might get something like this in the exam, and you'll need to pick out certain information from it. Most things you read have a lot of extra information to pad them out – and it's up to you to sift your way through this 'padding' to find the crucial information. It's rather like being a detective!

(?) Look at the leaflet and underline the words that you think are important. Then do the activity below and see if your underlined words are important or not.

38

> **REMEMBER**
> Don't worry if you don't understand all the words on the page. Pick out the key words.

Activités à Rouen

**Pour les enfants et jeunes (jusqu'à 16 ans)
du 19 juillet au 4 septembre**

Qu'est-ce qu'on peut faire à Rouen?

On peut:

▶ faire du sport (basketball, natation, escalade) ou visiter le zoo, les théâtres ou bien les musées. Il y a aussi des randonnées guidées dans la ville et ses environs.

▶ faire des excursions à la montagne en autobus ou par le train – chaque lundi: départ à 10h00.

▶ faire des activités au centre des jeunes. Par exemple, on peut faire de la photographie, dessiner, faire de la cuisine ou même danser.

▶ s'installer dans la salle technologique pour faire les jeux vidéos ou surfer sur l'Internet.

Bonnes vacances!

> Réservations pas toujours nécessaires.
> 34 rue Harnier, Rouen. Tél **43.23.43.56**

> **REMEMBER**
> You can make up your own activities on any French texts you've got – you could write out key words, make up questions or write a summary of it in English for extra practice.

◎ **Lis les phrases.** Read the statements.
Which activities in Rouen would you recommend for these people?

1 J'aime bien nager.
2 Je veux envoyer un télémessage à mon oncle en Amérique.
3 Ma mère m'a donné un appareil-photo pour mon anniversaire.
4 J'adore les animaux.

(?) Note down what you would recommend the people above to do. Start your sentences: **Tu peux ...**

Answering comprehension questions

You'll often get questions on a text in the reading exam, so you need to understand both the text itself and the questions. Let's check that you know the question words first of all!

◎ **Lis et relie.** Read and match the question words.

a Qui?	1 Who?
b Où?	2 What?
c Quand?	3 What?
d Comment?	4 When?
e Qu'est-ce que?	5 Why?
f Pourquoi?	6 How?
g Quel(le)?	7 Where?

! REMEMBER There's a fuller list of French questions on page 3.

Now here are some questions on the text from page 38. Read them through and see if you can understand them:

1 Qui peut faire toutes les activités?
2 Où est-ce qu'on peut faire les jeux vidéos?
3 Quand est-ce qu'on peut faire une excursion?
4 Comment va-t-on à la montagne?
5 Qu'est-ce qu'on peut faire au centre des jeunes? (2 choses)
6 Quel est le numéro de téléphone pour faire les réservations?
7 Est-ce qu'il faut toujours réserver?

! REMEMBER If the questions are in French, then you should answer them in French as well.

When you answer questions like these, you don't need to write full sentences – single words or short phrases will do.

h *Réponds aux questions ci-dessus.*

Practice activities

Learning vocabulary is something you've just got to do when you learn a language, but it needn't be a chore! You can find different ways of leaning words to make it more fun. Here are some ideas to get you started:

■ stick labels all around your home with French words on – **la télé** goes on the TV, **le lit** goes on your bed and **le chat** could even go on the cat's dish!

■ write words that you want to learn in a special book or file and keep them in your revision folder – look at the words now and again to remind yourself of them.

■ test yourself on ten words a day and give yourself one mark for each word that you remember – if you get ten marks, treat yourself to something nice!

■ make a wordsearch and put it in your folder. Look at it a week later – can you find the words? Say a sentence and/or ask a question with each word.

■ ask a friend or someone in the family to test you on your vocabulary lists – it doesn't matter if they don't speak French as they can give you the English word, you say the French word and they can check that's what is written on your list.

 # Writing

Writing specific words

Don't be put off by the thought of having to write French in the exam – some of the things you write will just be single words, short sentences or questions. You'll also get some help in the exam as you might have gaps to fill or words to re-order – just like in the next two activities!

(?) Think about your hobbies. Can you make a list of things you like doing? Start your sentences: **J'aime (bien) ...** or **Je fais ...** or **J'adore ...** or **Quelquefois ...**

◎ **Remplis les blancs.** Fill in the gaps.

REMEMBER Try to check your written answers in a dictionary or in the answer section at the back of this book – then you'll get your spellings correct.

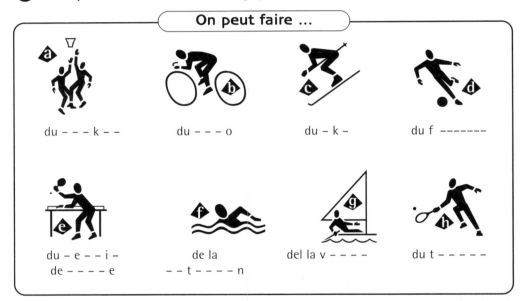

On peut faire ...

du – – – k – –   du – – – o   du – k –   du f – – – – – – –

du – e – – i –   de la   del la v – – – –   du t – – – – –
de – – – – e   – – t – – – – n

◎ **Ecris ces questions.** Write these questions.

REMEMBER Don't forget to learn the questions as well as the answers!

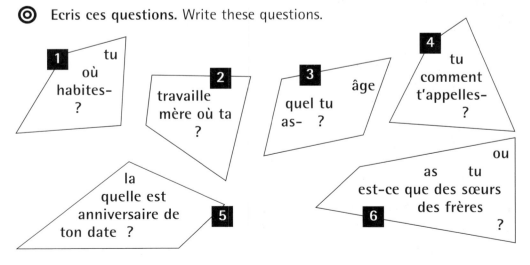

1 tu où habites- ?

2 travaille mère où ta ?

3 quel tu as- ? âge

4 tu comment t'appelles- ?

5 la quelle est anniversaire de ton date ?

6 as tu est-ce que des sœurs des frères ou ?

(?) Can you now write answers for these questions?

Filling in an ID form

The writing exam isn't just about writing! You'll also need to read French so that you know what you're being asked to write. Filling in an ID form is an example of this and you might get a similar form in the exam, so look carefully at the headings and make sure you know what they mean. Don't spend too long worrying about your answers being 100% accurate – if you can't remember exactly how tall you are, it doesn't matter – just put in a measurement that shows you understand that **taille** means 'height'.

◎ **Remplis le formulaire.** Fill in the form.

1 Nom de famille: _____

2 Prénom: _____

3 Adresse (avec code postal): _____

_____

4 Nationalité: _____

5 Age: _____   10 Passe-temps: _____

6 Date de naissance: _____   _____

7 Cheveux: _____   _____

8 Yeux: _____   _____

9 Taille: _____   _____

! R E M E M B E R
Don't lose marks by missing out bits of information. For example, remember to put in a postcode where it says **avec code postal** to show that you've understood.

Now you've just written short answers on the form, you can use the same information to write full sentences. This will help you to remember the words as you write them down again.

◎ **Copie et complète les phrases.** Copy and complete the sentences.

1 Je m'appelle …
2 Mes parents s'appellent …
3 J'habite …
4 Mon numéro de téléphone, c'est le …
5 J'ai … ans.
6 Mon anniversaire, c'est le …
7 J'ai des cheveux … et des yeux …
8 Mes passe-temps préférés sont …

! R E M E M B E R
Take care when copying that you get the spellings right.

Once you've written the sentences, put your work in your revision file so that you can revise from it nearer to the exam.

(?) Can you find out enough details from a friend so that you can make an ID form for them like the one above?

Writing

Replying to a letter

In this activity, you have to write a reply to a letter. You won't find the questions with the activity instructions this time – you'll have to read the letter, find the information asked for and then write a reply.

(?) What does Georges want to know? Find his questions in the letter and underline or highlight them.

(h) *Ecris une lettre à Georges. Réponds à ses questions.*

! REMEMBER Follow the layout of the example letter – the date goes on the top right-hand side and you start with **Cher** for a boy and **Chère** for a girl. Finish your letter in the same way: **A bientôt!**

> Dieppe, le 4 mai
>
> Chère Sylvie,
> Aujourd'hui je t'écris au sujet des passe-temps! Quels sont tes passe-temps préférés? Moi, j'aime bien aller au cinéma avec mes copains. J'aime aussi jouer au tennis le week-end. Quels sont tes sports préférés? Est-ce que tu fais de la natation en été?
> A bientôt
> *Georges*

Practice questions

Can you answer these questions – in writing?

Comment t'appelles tu? _____

Quels sont tes sports préférés? _____

Où habites-tu? _____

Quel pays voudrais-tu visiter? _____

Quel âge a ton/ta meilleur(e) ami(e)? _____

Où travaillent tes voisins? _____

(h) *Décris ta famille.*
Décris une vie très, très sportive.

Practice activity

Check to see how much you know!

Can you...

- write down four details about yourself?
- write down five sports?
- write down five other hobbies?
- write down seven questions to find out details about somebody else?
- write down four sentences about what there is (and is not) to do near you?

Exam focus: Using a dictionary

First of all, ask your teacher if you're allowed to use a dictionary in your exams. Make a note of the answer here:

	Dictionary	No dictionary
Listening exam	☐	☐
Speaking exam	☐	☐
Reading exam	☐	☐
Writing exam	☐	☐

So, now you know when you can use a dictionary, you need to know how to use it! First of all, get a French-English/English-French dictionary and a watch so you can time yourself on this next activity.

◎ **Cherche les mots dans un dictionnaire.** Look up the words in a dictionary.

piscine	bricolage	échecs	peinture	tambour
patin à glace	équitation	gagner	neveu	belle-sœur

| brother-in-law | neighbour | twin | spider | tortoise |

How long did that take you? Do you think you'll be able to look up that many words in your exams, or will it take too long? It's great to have a dictionary to refer to when you're doing French, but you mustn't be tempted to look up every word you don't know. You just won't have the time. That means that you'll have to choose words very carefully and look up only those ones that you really do need to do the activity. Of course, if you've spent a lot of time revising and learning vocabulary, you'll have less need for a dictionary!

When you look up the French word for an English word you don't know, you might find more than one possibility. Look at this dictionary extract below for 'train'.

> train 1 [n] (a) (rail) train *m*; [underground] métro *m*.
> (b) (procession) file *f*. (c) (dress) traîne *f*. 2 [vt] (a) (instruct)
> former, instruire; [sport] entraîner. (b) [direct gun etc.] braquer.

◎ Choose the right word from above to fill in these gaps.

1 Je vais à l'école en [train] ....

2 [I train] .... *au centre des sports chaque week-end.*

3 La femme porte une grande [train] .... *à la fête.*

4 [He trains] .... *les soldats.*

⁇ Work with a friend. Have a book or newspaper open and select some words at random. Both of you read the sentence and look up the word you've chosen in a French dictionary. Have you both got the same French word? You can always check it with your teacher or French assistant.

! REMEMBER Make sure you know your alphabet – it'll make looking up words in a dictionary a lot quicker in the exam!

! REMEMBER When you look up a word in the English/French section of your dictionary, it's a good idea to double-check it in the French/English bit to make sure you've got the right word.

! REMEMBER Before the exam, it's useful to brainstorm some impressive sounding words and phrases and then look them up yourself in a dictionary so they're ready to use in your own speaking and writing. Try these to start off: In my opinion ..., Personally I think ..., Usually ..., Sometimes ...

This section is about

- Your town
- Finding the way
- Weather
- Shopping

This section is all about the world around you and that includes the place you live in, how you find your way around it, what the weather is like there and what sorts of things you go shopping for. These are all topics that you'll need to know about for your exam.

So what do you think you'd find in a French city (**dans une ville française**)? Do you think it would be very different from a British city? Well, all the cars would be driving on the right-hand side of the road, for a start! When you watch the video, look out for any key differences between France and Britain. You might be surprised how familiar it all looks – especially some of the shops! What about your town? What can young people, tourists or children do there? Have you got a cinema (**un cinéma**) or a cathedral (**une cathédrale**)? Once you've worked your way through this section, you'll be able to describe all the things to do and see in your home town! So start thinking now about what you'd like to say.

France has got a lot of big cities, just like Britain and maybe you've visited one of them already. Have you been to Paris? Or what about Bordeaux, Rouen or Lyon? If you've ever been on a day trip to Calais or Boulogne you might have gone to the shops (**les magasins**) – did you visit a baker's (**boulangerie**) or were you more interested in looking at the clothes shops (**les boutiques**)? If you did make a visit,

then be prepared to talk about it in the exam and show off your expertise. In the exam, you might have to do a role play in a French shop, so listen carefully to how the people ask for various items – and how much they all cost!

If you go shopping in France, you can't use the Euro yet! You'll still have to use the French currency – the franc (**le franc**). There are 100 centimes to a franc, so you'll probably get some of them in your small change! Ask your teacher or parents or look in a newspaper to find out how many francs there are to a pound – then you can work out how much the things in the video cost in British money

If you visit a French city, then you'll have to get a map (**un plan**) so you can make your way to the different places. But what do you do if you get completely lost and even the map can't help you? You just ask for the way: **Pour aller ...?/Excusez-moi, où se trouve ...?** Once you've listened to the video and done the activities in this book, you'll be able to give and understand a lot of directions – so if a French person (or the examiner!) asks you the way to the station (**la gare**) you'll know exactly what to say.

In this section, you'll also find out how to talk about the weather – and that's a very popular subject with everybody!

So let's get started – **allons-y!**

InfoZONE

◎ These phrases will be really useful for your exam, so see if you can try and learn them!

Your town

J'habite une ville/un village.
    I live in a town/a village.

Il y a un cinéma/un marché/une gare ...
    There's a cinema/a market/a station ...

On trouve une piscine/des magasins ...
    You find a pool/some shops ...

On voit le château/le musée ...
    You see the castle/the museum ...

Nous avons un hôpital/une église ...
    We've got a hospital/a church ...

Ma ville est historique/belle/super ...
    My town is historic/lovely/super ...

J'aime habiter ici parce que c'est tranquille.
    I like living here because it's quiet.

Je le déteste parce que c'est ennuyeux.
    I hate it because it's boring.

Finding the way

Excusez-moi, où se trouve ...?
    Excuse me, where's ...?

Pour aller au/à la/à l'/aux ...?
    How do I get to...?

Est-ce qu'il y a ... près d'ici?
    Is there a ... near here?

Traversez la rue/le pont.   Cross the
    road/bridge.

Tournez à droite/à gauche.   Turn right/left.

Continuez tout droit.   Carry straight on.

Prenez la première rue à droite.
    Take the first road on the right.

Prenez la deuxième rue à gauche.
    Take the second road on the left.

C'est en face de la banque/la bibliothèque ...
    It's opposite the bank/the library ...

C'est près de la place.   It's near the square.

C'est à côté du parc.   It's next to the park.

C'est loin d'ici?   Is it far from here?

Weather

Quel temps fait-il?
    What's the weather like?

Il fait chaud/froid.   It's hot/cold.

Il fait beau/mauvais.   It's good/bad.

Il pleut/neige.   It's raining/snowing.

Il y a du vent/du soleil.   It's windy/sunny.

Il y a des nuages.   It's cloudy.

Shopping

Vous désirez?   What would you like?

Je voudrais des oranges/pommes/bananes ...
    I'd like some oranges/apples/bananas ...

Une/un ... s'il vous plaît.   A ... please.

C'est tout?   Is that everything?

C'est tout, merci.   That's all, thanks.

Ça fait combien?   How much is that?

Ça fait ... francs.   That's ... francs.

J'achète des tomates/pommes de terre ...
    I'm buying tomatoes/potatoes ...

Je vais aller au marché/à la boulangerie ...
    I'm going to go to the market/baker ...

C'est trop grand/petit/cher/lourd ...
    It's too big/small/expensive/heavy ...

Est-ce que je peux essayer ...?   Can I try ...?

le pantalon, la chemise, le jean, la robe
    trousers, shirt, jeans, dress

le pullover, la jupe, le blouson, la cravate
    jumper, skirt, jacket, tie

les chaussures, les chaussettes, les bottes
    shoes, socks, boots

Quelle couleur/taille?   What colour/size?

The World Around Us

45

BITESIZEfrench

Listening

Places in town

In the next couple of activities, you're going to focus on people talking about their town and what there is to see.

(?) How many 'town' words do you know? Play the video clips where people are talking about their home town and see how many of the words you recognise already.

Now play the clip of the young girl talking about her town in Guadelupe, and do the following activity.

◎ **Ecoute. Qu'est-ce qu'il y a dans la ville? Coche les bons mots.** Listen. What is there in the town? Tick the correct words.

Les magasins	**Un théâtre**	**Un marché**
Deux statues	**Un temple**	**Un port**
Un cinéma	**Un château**	**Une place**
Les cafés	**Une cathédrale**	**Une mairie**

REMEMBER When you've got to tick words that you hear and they're not in the right order (like here), it might be quicker to jot down an abbreviation for each place you hear and then tick it on the exam paper afterwards. For example, you could jot down **mag** for **magasins** and **chat** for **château**.

In the next clip, you'll hear people talking about Dijon and you then have to tick the statements that apply to the city. Use your common sense – you might know that Dijon is a big French city, so you could start off by ticking the statements that apply to any big city.

Dijon

1 *Il y a beaucoup de monuments.* ☐
2 *Pour les gens il n'y a rien à faire.* ☐
3 *Dijon est une ville très pauvre.* ☐
4 *On peut aller voir un opéra.* ☐
5 *Ici, on trouve un Arc de Triomphe.* ☐
6 *A Dijon on peut faire des courses.* ☐
7 *Il n'y a pas de cafés au centre-ville.* ☐
8 *A Dijon on peut bien dîner.* ☐

REMEMBER Read any French words on the exam paper that you might hear and think about how they sound.

Now find the clip where people are talking about Dijon and listen to check your answers.

◎ **Ecoute et coche les bonnes cases.** Listen and tick the correct boxes.

Tracing directions as you listen

In the next two activities you're going to hear directions – and that's a common exam activity.

(?) Before you listen to the video, check that you know the French words for 'left', 'right' and 'straight on'. Then think about how you would give directions to the places marked on the three maps below.

Now look at these three maps. You're going to have to choose the correct map to match the directions you hear. Don't just assume it's map a) when you hear the word **la rue en face** – you've got to listen to the complete direction before you can decide which map is correct.

! REMEMBER Make abbreviated notes as you listen for the first time. Then check your notes against the maps to find the correct one. On the second listening, trace the directions on your chosen map as you listen to check you've got the right one.

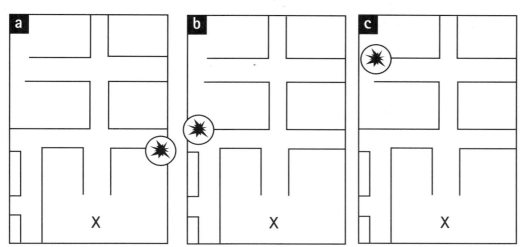

Find the clip where a man with a map asks the question: **Où se trouve le quartier de la petite France, s'il vous plaît?** and do the following activity.

◎ Ecoute et coche le bon plan. Listen and tick the correct map (above).

Now find the clip where another man asks a woman the question: **Est-ce qu'il y a un bureau de change près d'ici?** and do the following activity.

◎ Ecoute. Quel numéro est le bureau de change? Listen. What number is the bureau de change?

If you want, you can trace the route on the map with a pencil to help you to find the place you're looking for.

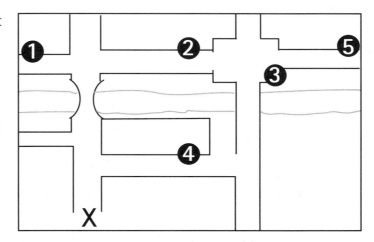

The World Around Us

●●● 📺 Listening

Multiple choice – shopping

One thing that you're bound to hear in a shopping dialogue is prices and that means numbers! You can check your numbers on page 49 if you need to.

(?) Take a look at these multiple choice questions and see if you can work out what you're going to be listening to later.

! **REMEMBER** Read every answer very carefully. Sometimes they're very similar, like 1a and 1b so it's important that you don't confuse them and tick the wrong box.

1 La première femme a acheté:
- [ ] *a un short pour la fête*
- [ ] *b un short pour l'été*
- [ ] *c un short pour son enfant.*

2 La deuxième femme a acheté:
- [ ] *a un jean et une chemise*
- [ ] *b deux jeans et une robe*
- [ ] *c un jean pour son mari.*

3 La jeune fille a acheté:
- [ ] *a une jupe d'été*
- [ ] *b une chemise d'été*
- [ ] *c une robe d'été.*

4 La casquette de sa copine:
- [ ] *a a coûté 96 francs*
- [ ] *b a coûté 67 francs*
- [ ] *c a coûté 69 francs.*

5 La robe de la femme est:
- [ ] *a marron*
- [ ] *b rouge*
- [ ] *c bleue.*

6 L'homme a acheté:
- [ ] *a des chaussures*
- [ ] *b des chaussettes*
- [ ] *c un pantalon.*

7 Le dernier homme a acheté:
- [ ] *a un pullover blanc*
- [ ] *b un pullover vert*
- [ ] *c un pullover rouge.*

8 Le pullover:
- [ ] *a a coûté 249 francs*
- [ ] *b a coûté 49 francs*
- [ ] *c a coûté 349 francs.*

! **REMEMBER** Check all your answers through when the tape is played for the second time – have you really ticked the correct box each time?

Now play the clip in Marks & Spencer and do the multiple choice activity.

◎ **Ecoute et coche les bonnes cases.** Listen and tick the correct boxes.

Practice activity

Listening to things over and over again (and saying them to yourself) while you're revising helps to make the words and sounds stick in your mind.

Even if you're not actually doing the listening activities in this book, you can play the video itself and get used to the sounds and phrases in it.

Concentrate on a different section each week and just play it as often as you can –

you could have it on in the background while you're tidying your room or having breakfast or just watch it for a few minutes before you go to school every day.

As the week goes on, see how much of the video you start to recognise and how many sentences or words you can say before the speakers do.

Listening to the video once just isn't enough!

Exam focus: Knowing your numbers

Numbers come up all over the place, so it's important that you know how to say them and you know what they sound like in French! For example, you might have to give a phone number, give your house number, your age, ask for a certain number of items in a shop, ask for a bus number, talk about money ... the list goes on and on!

(?) Can you say five French sentences with numbers in them?

Numbers to 20

You probably learned your numbers when you started French lessons, so now's the time to revise them properly and make sure that you're confident with them.

◎ **Trouve les numéros et fais une liste.** Find the numbers and make a list.

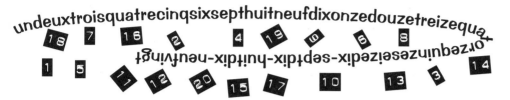

> ! **REMEMBER**
> You don't have to revise all your numbers at once. Keep coming back to this page in a spare moment to check you remember them all OK!

Numbers 21–99

These higher numbers take a bit more remembering, but see if you can try and learn them all the same.

◎ **Fais correspondre les numéros aux mots.** Match the numbers to the words.

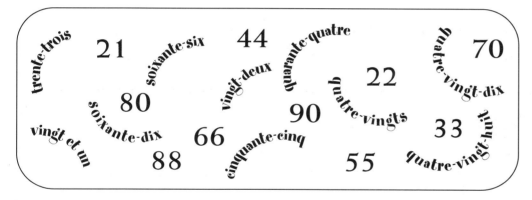

Whenever you see a number – on a signpost, a book, a CD or a car for example – try and say it to yourself in French. If you can't remember the number, then check it on this page as soon as you can.

> ! **REMEMBER**
> Don't worry about the spelling of numbers too much, as you can always write them as figures – '7', '63', '234' etc.

Higher numbers

A couple of useful higher numbers to remember are **cent** (hundred) and **mille** (thousand).

The World Around Us

Talking about your town

In the speaking exam, it's good if you can answer questions and say things in full sentences. There's nothing wrong with giving a one-word answer, but you'll score more marks if you can give full answers.

In the next activity, you're going to be asked what there is to see in your town. Let's see if we can work out how to answer in a full sentence.

First of all look at these English words – can you say them in French?

Exemple: – *Théâtre.*
– *Un théâtre.*

1 a theatre
2 a station
3 a cinema
4 a museum

5 a hospital
6 a castle
7 some shops
8 a swimming pool

Now you can try and say full sentences with those words.

Say full sentences, using the places above 1–8. Look at the example first – this will help you as you speak. All you have to do, is say **Il y a …** or **Nous avons …** and then add in a place each time.

Exemple: – Qu'est-ce qu'il y a dans ta ville?
– Il y a *un théâtre.*
– Nous avons *un théâtre.*

The next thing to do is to make your sentences even longer. That means giving more details about the town, or even giving an opinion about it.

Réponds aux questions. Answer the questions.
The ideas in the boxes below might help you.

Exemple: – Qu'est-ce qu'il y a dans ta ville?
– Il y a *un grand cinéma.* C'est vraiment *super.*
– Il y a *une piscine.* Mais elle est très *vieille* et *sale.*
– Qu'est-ce qu'on peut faire dans ta ville?
– On peut *faire une promenade dans le parc.* J'aime beaucoup faire ça quand *il fait beau.*

lots of shops – expensive	sports centre – very small	cafés – no young people there	visit the castle – beautiful	swim in the lake – when it's hot	go to the theatre – boring

In the exam, you'll be asked to talk for a few minutes on a certain topic – and that might be your town. Prepare a short talk about your town – using full sentences, of course! Record what you say on to tape – you can then revise from your tape before the exam.

REMEMBER
Speak as clearly as possible.

REMEMBER
You don't always have to give positive opinions when you're talking in French – you can also say negative things!

50

Giving directions

(?) In this activity, you'll be asking for the way to various places. Before you start, say the words below out loud in French.

1 the post office
2 the university
3 the underground station
4 the supermarket
5 the stadium
6 the town hall

Did you have to use your dictionary to say some of those words? Now ask how to get to those places. You could start each question with **Où se trouve ...?** The example will remind you as you speak – look at it first.

Exemple: – Excusez-moi, où se trouve *la poste?*

In the exam, there won't be a lot of English words giving you cues. Instead you'll often have pictures and symbols that signal what you have to say.

(?) Look at these picture cues. What do you think you have to say for each one?

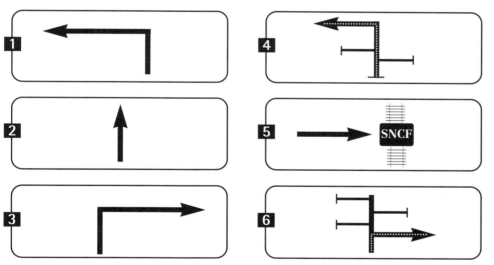

Don't worry if you're not sure what to say, as you can always look at the example to help you.

Exemple: – Excusez-moi, où se trouve *la poste?*
         – *Tournez à gauche.*

So in this activity, the picture cues are all answers to questions about finding places. The examiner will ask you a question, **Où se trouve ...?** and you look at the picture and give the answer.

⊙ **Regarde les images ci-dessus et donne les directions.** Look at the pictures above and give directions.

Exemple: – Excusez-moi, où se trouve *la poste?*
         – *Tournez à gauche.*

REMEMBER If there are any specific places near where you live (such as cliffs, a mosque, laboratories), then look the words up before the exam, so you can talk about them.

51

REMEMBER There's nearly always more than one way of saying things. For example, when you're asking the way to places, you can ask **Comment va-t-on au/à la ...?** as well as **Où est ...?** and even **C'est où, ...?**

REMEMBER Don't rush your answers – take your time to think them through!

The World Around Us

Speaking

Practising a shopping dialogue

In the next activity you'll be taking part in a dialogue. You'll do this kind of role play in your exam – your teacher or the examiner will ask the questions.

(?) To start with, look at the list on the right.
Can you say the words in French?

Exemple: – *Une bouteille d'eau minérale.*

You can use a dictionary to look up words if you like, but time will be precious in the exam, so don't spend too much time looking up words here.

◎ Now choose some of the items and make up a dialogue in a shop with them. Remember to look carefully at the example dialogue before you start – this will help you as you go along.

! REMEMBER
If you're doing a role play in a shop, be polite and say **bonjour Monsieur/Madame** and **au revoir Monsieur/Madame** to the sales person.

1 bottle of mineral water
2 cherry pie
3 four baguettes
4 some potatoes
5 five tomatoes
6 some coffee
7 a chicken
8 some ham

Exemple: – Bonjour Madame/Monsieur, vous désirez?
– Bonjour. Je voudrais *une tarte aux pommes*, s'il vous plaît.
– Voilà!
– Merci. Je voudrais aussi *une baguette.*
– C'est tout?
– Oui, c'est tout. Ça fait combien?
– Ça fait *quatre francs dix.*
– Merci. Au revoir.

Practice questions

Can you answer these questions?

Qu'est-ce qu'il y dans ta ville?
Exemple: *Il y a …*
Qu'est-ce que tu aimes acheter?
Exemple: *J'aime acheter …*

(b) *Décris ta ville.*

See how much you can remember!

Can you…

■   name six places in town?

■   explain how to get to school from your home?

■   ask for four items at the supermarket?

■   count in tens from ten to 100.

Practice activity

When you're next walking around your town, going to school or sitting on the bus, look around you. What can you see? Try to say the places in your head – in French, of course!

For extra practice, you could even try to record a tour guide on tape about the place where you live.

📺 In the video, you're often shown ways of making your answers to questions more interesting and a bit longer. To do this, the speakers often use adjectives (describing words). Have a look at these adjectives – do you know what they mean?

historique	*petit(e)*	*propre*
sale	*formidable*	*grand(e)*
intéressant(e)	*excellent(e)*	*bruyant(e)*

Do you know why some of the adjectives have got an 'e' in brackets? Well, do you remember how all nouns are either masculine or feminine (see page 25)? It's this that makes the adjectives in French change. Normally an adjective just adds an 'e' at the end when it's with a **la** (feminine) word. Take a look:

Le *village est* **grand.** **La** *ville est* **grande**.

What do you think happens to adjectives if they're with a **les** (plural) word? Take a look:

Les *villages sont* **grands.** **Les** *villes sont* **grandes**.

That's right – they add an 's' at the end!

◎ Fill in the gaps with the correct adjective from the box.

1 J'adore les jupes ....
2 La chemise est trop ....
3 Le jean est ....
4 Les pullovers sont trop ....

> petits
>   rouges
>   grande
>   bleu

📺 You probably noticed that some adjectives in the video didn't just add an 'e' for **la** words, but that they sounded quite different. Do you remember these sentences?

C'est une très **belle** *ville. La cathédrale est très* **vieille***. Les maisons sont* **belles** *et* **vieilles***.*

Those are irregular adjectives. Have a look at how some more of them work:

masculine	masculine plural		feminine	feminine plural
beau	beaux	⇨	belle	belles
vieux	vieux	⇨	vieille	vieilles
nouveau	nouveaux	⇨	nouvelle	nouvelles
bon	bons	⇨	bonne	bonnes
blanc	blancs	⇨	blanche	blanches
affreux	affreux	⇨	affreuse	affreuses

◎ Fill in the gaps with the correct form of the adjective.

1 Ma ville est très .... [old]
2 Le parc est .... [beautiful]
3 Les films sont toujours .... [good]
4 Les maisons sont .... [terrible]

If you want to find out more about grammar, ask your teacher or the BITESIZE on-line team to recommend a French grammar book for you – that way you can do more activities and get to know even more about the way the French language works.

Reading

Revising vocabulary

When you're revising French vocabulary, you don't always have to write lists of words with their English translations. You might find it a good idea to draw symbols or sketch pictures for the words instead to help you remember them. Have a go at drawing some pictures to help you remember directions.

◎ **Dessine une image pour chaque phrase.** Draw a picture for each phrase.

1 tournez à droite	2 tournez à gauche	3 continuez tout droit
4 traversez le pont	5 en face de l'église	6 à côté de la banque

REMEMBER You can use this strategy of drawing symbols/diagrams to help you learn vocabulary – you don't always have to write English/French lists of words and phrases.

Another way of revising vocabulary is to make up puzzles for a friend to do, or for you to do a few weeks later. You can write anagrams, do wordsearches or even make up crosswords. Here's a puzzle already made for you to do!

◎ **Fais le mot croisés.** Do the crossword.

1 On peut nager ici, même s'il pleut!

2 On trouve beaucoup d'argent ici.

3 On peut faire le plein à la station-...

4 La boulangerie, l'épicerie et la boutique, par exemple.

5 On y va si on est malade.

6 Ici on peut emprunter les livres.

7 Le train pour Paris part d'ici!

REMEMBER Get some extra help with your French revision via the BITESIZE internet service. The e-mail address is on the back of this book.

Weather and shopping

Now let's look at a couple of exam-style activities. In the first one, you've got to match weather types to symbols – make sure you look at the symbols carefully and don't confuse h (snow) for a (rain) when you write your answer.

◎ **Fais correspondre les mots (1–8) avec les symboles (a–h).** Match the words (1–8) to the symbols (a–h).

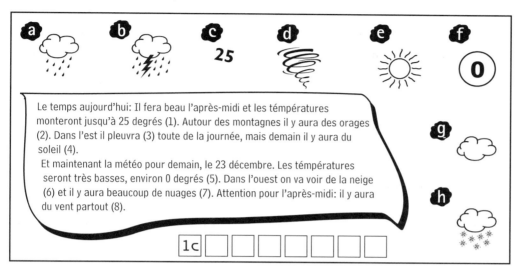

55

REMEMBER In the exam you won't get the instructions translated into English like you've got here – so it's important that you know the words. Look at page 3 for a list of instruction words.

Now you're going to put a dialogue in the right order. This time make sure that you don't throw marks away by writing your answer down wrong – tick off each speech bubble once you've put them in order to check that:
a) you've used all the speech bubbles and b) you haven't written down one of them twice by mistake.

◎ **Range les bulles.** Put the speech bubbles in the correct order.

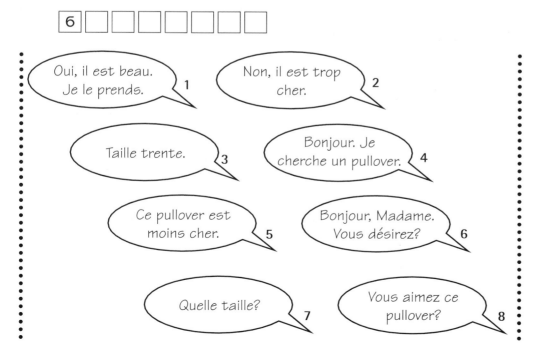

REMEMBER If you've got an example answer, use it to start you off – here you know what the first speech bubble is (6), so look at that one first and then look for the next one.

The World Around Us

A letter about town

◎ **Fais correspondre les mots (1–8) avec les images.** Match up the words (1–8) with the pictures (a–h).

! REMEMBER You can just pick out the key words here (i.e. the ones beside each number) – you don't need to read and understand the whole letter!

Valognes, le 5 février

Chère Monique,

Nous sommes enfin arrivés ici à Valognes, et notre appartement est super. Il y a beaucoup de choses à faire et je ne m'ennuie pas de tout. Mais mes copains me manquent, bien sûr!

En face de notre appartement il y a un grand parc (1) – c'est fantastique et j'y joue au football avec mon frère tous les soirs. Il gagne toujours! Il y a aussi une rivière (2) là-bas – hier j'y suis allé à la pêche, mais on n'a pas mangé de poisson le soir!

La ville est très vivante et il y a beaucoup de jeunes gens – au centre-ville il y a une grande rue piétonne (3), où se trouve tous les magasins et les cafés (4). On ne peut pas aller au centre-ville en voiture – il faut se garer dans un parking (5) en banlieue et prendre l'autobus.

Qu'est-ce qu'il y a encore dans ma ville? Et bien, on a la mairie (6) – elle est très vieille (presque 500 ans je crois) et il y a une belle église (7) sur la Grande Place. Il y a aussi un hôpital (8) – ma sœur y est en ce moment – elle s'est cassée une jambe!

A bientôt!

Oliver

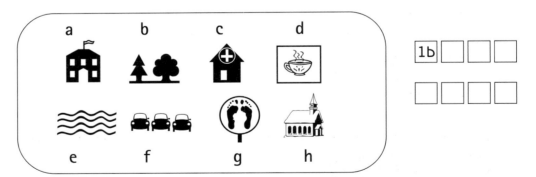

1b ☐ ☐ ☐
☐ ☐ ☐ ☐

! REMEMBER If the question specifies the number of things you need to mention in your answer (i.e. **2 choses** in question 4) make sure you write down that amount to get full marks.

ℎ *Lis la lettre et réponds aux questions.*

1 Où habite Oliver?
2 Qu'est-ce qu'il fait dans le parc?
3 Qu'est-ce qu'il fait à la rivière?
4 Qu'est-ce qu'il y a dans la rue piétonne (2 choses)?
5 Où se trouve le parking?
6 Elle est comment, la mairie?
7 Pourquoi la sœur d'Oliver, est-elle à l'hôpital?

A supermarket leaflet

Some of the reading matter in the exam will be 'realia' – that means things like real magazine articles, adverts, food wrappings and signs from France. Don't worry about them though, as you'll often only need to understand a few of the words and there might also be pictures to help you. Some of the words in adverts and signs might be trade names, brand names or place names, so it's important that you try to focus on the actual French words you need.

(?) Have a look at this shopping brochure. Can you highlight all the French words on it for things you can eat? Ignore everything else.

Raisin de table [1kg]	5F70	Verres [6 bleu/rouge]	34F
Disques p. l'ordinateur [10] –	65F	Tartes aux fraises	14F
Pâtes (toutes varietés)	3F40	Yaourt aux fruits 200g carton	9F50
Côtelette de porc [1kg]	12F80	Lave-vaisselle Nouvel	10F50
Dentifrice Teramed	7F20	Baguette	5F10
Saucissons [10]	28F	Beurre de Normandie [250g]	8F60
Haricots verts	5F45	Sauce tomate (en bouteille)	7F30
Chaussettes (bleues/noires)	13F	*Le shopping – c'est bon!*	

◎ **Qu'est-ce qu'on ne doit pas acheter pour ces gens?** What shouldn't you buy for these people? Choose something from the brochure above.

1 Je suis végétarien!
2 Je suis allergique au lait.
3 Je mange tout! Mais je déteste les légumes!
4 Je n'aime pas les choses sucrées.

! REMEMBER In this activity you need to choose things you would <u>not</u> buy for the people. Don't miss words like **ne ... pas**.

The World Around Us

Practice activity

Don't forget to learn the French instructions for the exam activities as well as the topic areas themselves – if you can't understand what to do, you won't be able to show off your French to the examiners!

Try and learn or revise two instructions from page 3 each time you work with this book.

Make a list here of four key instructions you want to learn:

1 _____

2 _____

3 _____

4 _____

Writing

Writing specific words

◎ Ecris les mots. Write down the words. They're all items of clothing.

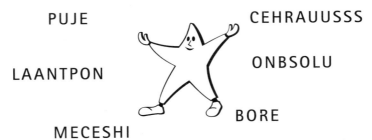

PUJE

CEHRAUUSSS

LAANTPON

ONBSOLU

BORE

MECESHI

Have you written the words down with **le** and **la**? Check on page 94 to see if you've got the right word.

❔ Now think about what you wear. What do you like wearing to school? And to the disco? Make a list of other clothing words.

In the exam, you might get a map or a picture to write about. The instruction will tell you exactly what you need to write, so make sure you read it carefully and don't just start writing any old thing about the picture! For example, in this next activity, you've got to write directions from the bus stop to your home. There's no point writing directions from your home to the bus stop – even if the French is correct, you won't get marks because you haven't answered the question.

◎ **Un copain va te rendre visite. Il va prendre l'autobus. Ecris les directions de l'arrêt d'autobus à ta maison.**

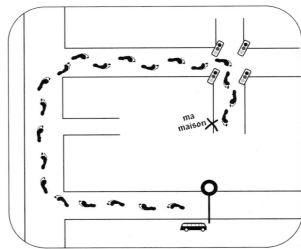

A good way of revising is to practise, practise and practise again! Once you've done an activity here and checked your answer at the back, you can write your own pieces of French. For example, you could write directions from your house to school or from the library to the cinema. Show your work to your teacher or French assistant, or e-mail the BITESIZE team to check that you're getting it right.

> ❗ **REMEMBER** You may need to understand the names of all sorts of clothes in the exam, so the more you learn now, the more you'll recognise when you're in the exam!

> ❗ **REMEMBER** Draft notes in rough first. Try to give as much information as you can in your answer.

Writing lists

In the exam, you might have to write a list of five or six words – for example, a shopping list, a list of what you're wearing or a list of places in town. Make sure you go into the exam full of ideas for this kind of task.

◎ **Qu'est-ce qu'il y a dans ta ville? Fais une liste (7 choses).** What is there in your town? Make a list (7 things).

1 _____
2 _____
3 _____
4 _____
5 _____
6 _____
7 _____

❗ REMEMBER Never leave an answer line blank – even if you're not 100% sure of how to spell the word, it's better to have a go, rather than not write anything.

The 'Practice activity' at the end of each Writing section in this book gives you ideas for writing lists on your GCSE topics – once you've written them, put them in your revision file and try to keep revising them before the exam.

Practice questions

Can you answer these questions – in writing?

Qu'est-ce qu'il y a dans ta ville? _____

_____

Aimes-tu habiter dans ta ville? Pourquoi? _____

Qu'est-ce que tu portes: au collège? _____

à la maison? _____

h *Décris une ville idéale pour les jeunes.*

Practice activity

Check to see how much you know!

Can you...

- write down six items of clothing?
- write down four directions?
- list six places in town?

The World Around Us

The World of Work

This section is about

- Jobs

- Future plans

- Adverts

- Using the phone

This section is all about the world of work and that includes jobs, careers and your plans and hopes for the future – advertising and using the phone are also covered. These are all topics that you'll need to know about for your exam.

So what about you? What do you think you want to do later on in life – **Que penses-tu faire comme métier plus tard**? This section will help you to talk about your future plans and what you think is important. Maybe you want to go to university – **Je veux aller à l'université**. Or are you interested in working in a bank? **Je voudrais travailler dans une banque**. Have you started to think about possible jobs yet? You could be a teacher (**professeur**), a mechanic (**mécanicien(ne)**), a doctor (**médecin**) ... the choice is yours!

In this section you'll also see three French adverts (**les publicités**) – see what you think about them! Maybe you've already seen some French adverts on satellite or cable TV – do you think they're better than the ones on TV here? Watching TV adverts helps to make learning French fun! Later in the video, some pupils give their opinions on adverts – listen out carefully for what they say, as you'll be expected to give your opinion on things in the exam, so their ideas might help you.

And what about talking on the phone? Can you ring somebody up and speak in French?

Some people find talking on the phone scarier than talking face to face, but this section will provide you with the key phrases you need to make a phone call go smoothly – and you might just have to use them in the exam! Would you recognise a public phone in France? The photo below shows you what they look like, so if you ever go to France you'll know where to phone from!

So let's get started – **allons-y!**

🎯 These phrases will be really useful for your exam, so see if you can try and learn them!

Jobs

Je suis/Il/Elle est ...   I'm a/He/She is a ...

Je suis directeur/directrice.   I'm a director.

l'agent de police, le dentiste, l'ingénieur   police officer, dentist, engineer

le professeur, la secrétaire, le médecin   teacher, secretary, doctor

le coiffeur/la coiffeuse, le facteur/la factrice   hairdresser, postman/woman

l'infirmier/l'infirmière, l'électricien(ne)   nurse, electrician

Que font tes parents/copains?   What do your parents/friends do?

Que fait ta sœur/ton frère?   What does your sister/brother do?

Je travaille dans une banque/une usine ...   I work in a bank/a factory ...

Il travaille dans un bureau/un magasin ...   He works in an office/a shop ...

Elle travaille dans un garage/à la maison ...   She works in a garage/at home ...

J'aime mon travail.   I like my job.

C'est passionnant/intéressant/varié.   It's exciting/interesting/varied.

C'est difficile/stressant/fatigant/facile.   It's difficult/stressful/tiring/easy.

Je travaille entre sept heures et neuf heures.   I work between seven and nine o'clock.

Future plans

Que penses-tu faire comme métier plus tard?   What job do you think you'll do later?

Je voudrais être ...   I'd like to be ...

Je vais étudier.   I'm going to study.

Je ne sais pas (ce que je voudrais faire).   I don't know (what I want to do).

Je voudrais avoir un contact avec les gens.   I'd like to work with other people.

Ce qui est important pour moi, c'est de faire quelque chose que j'aime.   The important thing for me is to do something that I enjoy.

Il faut aimer son travail pour bien le faire.   You have to like your job to do it well.

Il faut que le travail m'intéresse.   The work has to interest me.

Adverts

Comment trouves-tu cette publicité?   What do you think of this advert?

Je la trouve très originale et amusante.   I think it's very original and amusing.

Elle était un peu démodée/drôle/moche ...   It was a bit old-fashioned/funny/awful ...

ennuyeux/ennuyeuse, formidable, chouette   boring, great, excellent

J'ai trouvé ... vraiment génial/nul.   I found ... really great/rubbish.

A mon avis, c'était (extrêmement) ...   In my opinion, it was (extremely) ...

Using the phone

Allô, Christophe?   Hello, is that Christophe?

Salut, c'est ... à l'appareil.   Hello, it's ... speaking.

Allô, est-ce que je peux parler à ...?   Hello, can I talk to ...?

Je suis désolé(e), mais ... n'est pas là.   I'm sorry, but ... isn't here.

Je peux laisser un message?   Can I leave a message?

Je rappellerai plus tard.   I'll ring again later.

Ne quittez pas.   Don't hang up.

61

The World of Work

Listening

Predicting what you might hear

Before you listen to a video clip or the tape in the exam, it's a good idea to think about a few words you might hear first.

(?) Look at these English words for jobs and see if you know what words you might hear on the video. Say them out loud or in your head.

train driver
teacher
banker
doctor
unemployed

62

REMEMBER You can use the video to extend your vocabulary – listen to all the clips about jobs and make a list of the words for jobs – how many can you find? Check the spellings in a dictionary.

Now find the clip where five people reply to the question: **Quel est votre travail?** and do the activity.

◎ **Ecoute et écris le métier de chaque personne.** Listen and write down each person's job.

1 La première femme est ....
2 La fille est ....
3 Le premier homme est ....
4 Le deuxième homme est ....
5 Le dernier homme est ....

(?) In the next clip, some people are giving their opinions about their jobs – can you hear any negative opinions?

Now play the clip where people are talking about their working hours and do the activity below. If you need extra practice of times at this point, look at page 15.

REMEMBER When you listen for the first time, jot down notes and then fill in the answers on the answer sheet afterwards. On the second listening, look at your chosen answer for each number and check it against what you hear. You can always change your mind and cross out your answer and correct it if you need to.

◎ **Ecoute et coche la bonne heure.** Listen and tick the correct time.

1	**08:00**	**08:30**	**08:15**	**09:00**
2	**10:00**	**08:30**	**08:00**	**09:00**
3	**07:00**	**08:30**	**18:00**	**19:00**
4	**07:00**	**17:00**	**19:15**	**20:00**
5	**16:25**	**14:25**	**15:20**	**16:40**
6	**19:00**	**13:00**	**09:30**	**20:00**
7	**22:10**	**23:00**	**22:00**	**10:30**

Listening to people talking about jobs

You don't always have to listen out for specific words to get the marks in the exam – sometimes you can just get the gist of what the people say or catch a couple of words that give you the answer. The following activity is an example of that. You've got to match words to phrases as you listen – but you don't have to understand everything the people say.

First look at the words and phrases and say them out loud to yourself – then you'll know what to listen out for once the video starts.

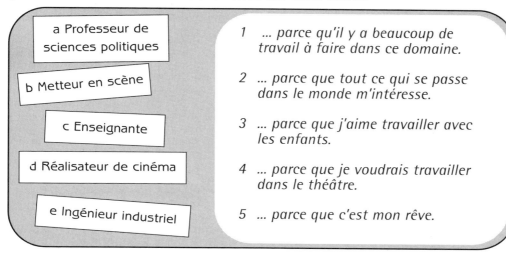

a Professeur de sciences politiques

b Metteur en scène

c Enseignante

d Réalisateur de cinéma

e Ingénieur industriel

1   ... parce qu'il y a beaucoup de travail à faire dans ce domaine.

2   ... parce que tout ce qui se passe dans le monde m'intéresse.

3   ... parce que j'aime travailler avec les enfants.

4   ... parce que je voudrais travailler dans le théâtre.

5   ... parce que c'est mon rêve.

! REMEMBER You can start anticipating the answers before the tape starts – for example, which of the phrases (1–5) do you think is most likely to go with **Enseignante (c)**?

Find the clip where some teenagers reply to the question: **Quel métier penses-tu faire plus tard?** and do this activity.

◎ **Ecoute et fais correspondre les métiers aux phrases.** Listen and match the jobs to the sentences (above).

In the exam you might have to listen and write in specific words in sentences or texts. That means that you've got to listen very carefully for individual words. The first thing to do, of course, is to read the gapped text so you can familiarise yourself with what you'll hear once the tape starts.

(?) Read these gapped sentences. Can you work out what you're going to be listening for?

1 La seule chose importante pour moi, c'est de faire quelque chose que ....

2 Il faut qu'on .... son travail pour .... le faire.

3 Pour moi, c'est important d'avoir .... avec les gens.

4 Il faut choisir un métier qui va nous intéresser pendant ....

5 J'ai besoin d'un travail qui m'...................

! REMEMBER You might not always hear these gapped sentences exactly as they are printed here – so be prepared for a few differences. But you will hear all the information you need to fill each gap.

The World of Work

Now play the clip where five people reply to the question: **Quels sont les critères dans le choix de métier?** and do this activity.

◎ **Ecoute et remplis les blancs.** Listen and fill in the gaps (above).

 **Listening**

Multiple choice – adverts

An important thing to remember in the exam, is not to panic – that won't get you anywhere! Activities like the next one might look scary, but once you start them, you'll be able to cope. Just take a deep breath, relax and tackle the activity bit by bit!

Find the clips with the three adverts and do this activity.

◎ **Ecoute et coche les bonnes cases.** Listen and tick the correct boxes.

64

! REMEMBER In the exam, you'll hear the tape recording twice only – while you're revising, you can listen as often as you like!

1 La première publicité, c'est pour
     a quelque chose à manger ☐
     b quelque chose à boire ☐
     c quelque chose à porter. ☐

2 La deuxième publicité, c'est pour
     a une école ☐
     b une boisson ☐
     c quelque chose de sucré. ☐

3 Dans ce produit, il y a
     a du fromage ☐
     b du poisson ☐
     c du chocolat. ☐

! REMEMBER Make sure you tick the right box in activities like this – don't throw marks away by ticking box b instead of box a by mistake.

4 La troisième publicité, c'est pour
     a la crème ☐
     b le dentifrice ☐
     c les dentistes. ☐

5 On peut
     a boire ce produit ☐
     b voir et sentir ce produit ☐
     c jouer avec ce produit. ☐

Practice activity

When you've got a spare moment, put the French video on and play a clip that you find particularly interesting – or one that covers the topic area you're revising at the time. Listen and watch the clip through once and note down any key words you'd like to learn. Then rewind the tape and play the clip again – but this time with the volume turned right down. Pause the tape every so often and say a sentence or phrase to describe what you can see or what's happening. Then carry on like this, pausing and speaking and then continuing.

You can then watch the clip again at the end with the volume turned up and see how much you remembered or compare the things that you said with the actual French speakers.

GrammarZONE

📺 Do you remember when to use **tu** and **vous**? Here's a clue: the interviewer always addresses the younger pupils as **tu** and the adults as **vous**. So, let's recap:

tu ⇨ a child, a friend, a member of your family (and an animal)
vous ⇨ an adult or adults

◎ How would you address the following people? Write **tu** or **vous** next to them.

1 le prof de français ....
2 le voisin, M. Brun ....
3 l'enfant de Mme. Jacques ....
4 ma meilleure amie ....
5 Tante Françoise ....
6 le père de Marc ....

📺 In the video, the interviewer asked young people several questions. Look at these two:

Quel travail fait ta mère?   Que fait ton frère?

Do you notice how there are two words for 'your' in those examples? What are they? Just like there are three words for 'the' (**le**, **la** and **les**) and two words for 'a' (**un** and **une**), so there are three words for 'your' and 'my' etc. Let's have a look at them:

Mon *père travaille à la banque.*
Ma *mère est professeur.*
Mes **grandparents** *ne travaillent pas.*

Can you work out the pattern in those sentences? Look at this table for some extra help:

	the	my	your	his/her
masculine words	le	mon	ton	son
feminine words	la	ma	ta	sa
plural words	les	mes	tes	ses
words starting with a vowel	l'	mon	ton	son

◎ Fill in the gaps with the correct word for 'my', 'your' (**tu**) or 'his/her'.

1 J'ai un frère et une sœur. .... frère est prof et .... sœur est médecin.
2 M. Château aime beaucoup .... nouvelle voiture.
3 Où habites-tu? Elle est grande, ... maison?
4 Clémentine adore .... père.

📺 And what about saying 'your' when you're addressing somebody as **vous**? And how do you say 'our' and 'their'? Here are some more sentences from the video to help you:

Quel métier fait votre père?   Que font vos enfants?

Can you see the words for 'your' in those sentences? Look at this table for some extra help:

	the	your	our	their
all singular words	le/la/l'	votre	notre	leur
all plural words	les	vos	nos	leurs

◎ Fill in the gaps with the correct word for 'our', 'your' (**vous**) or 'their'.

1 Avez-vous écrit des cartes postales à .... copains?
2 Nous nettoyons .... chambre chaque week-end.
3 Ils ont trouvé .... affaires dans le lac.
4 Jean et Julie n'aiment pas .... prof d'anglais.

Speaking

66

! **REMEMBER** When you talk about jobs in French, you don't have to use the French for 'a': **Je suis professeur** means 'I'm <u>a</u> teacher'.

Building on one word answers

You're going to be asked about the jobs you'd like to do next, so let's start with some French words for a few jobs.

(?) Can you say these jobs out loud?

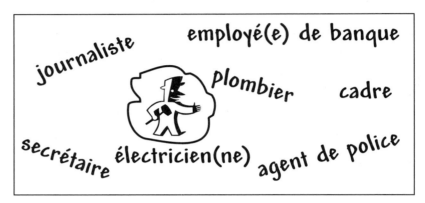

Now you can use these jobs to talk about what you'd like to do. Choose as many jobs from the box as you like. Look at the examples before you begin - try not to stick to the same example every time, but experiment to make your answers as detailed as possible.

◎ **Réponds à la question.** Answer the question.

Exemple: – Que penses-tu faire comme métier plus tard?
– Bien, *plombier*.
– Je voudrais être *cadre*.
– Je vais travailler comme *sécretaire*.
– Je vais aller à l'université pour étudier. Après ça je vais être *journaliste pour un journal.*

Now you can build your answers up even more and really impress the examiner! Do you remember the easiest way of doing that? Yes, by giving your opinion and some extra details.

(?) Can you say some longer sentences about jobs? You can use the ideas in the boxes to help you with some ideas, if you like.

! **REMEMBER** There are two words for a lot of jos in French! One is for a man and one is for a woman: **le directeur** (director/ headmaster) and **la directrice** (director/ headmistress).

Exemple: – Je ne voudrais pas être médecin, parce que c'est un métier trop fatigant et je déteste les hôpitaux!
– J'aimerais bien être acteur/actrice, parce que c'est un métier très intéressant et j'adore le théâtre.

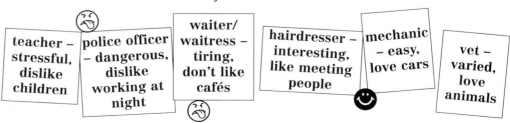

Speaking on the phone

You might have to do a role play in the exam where you're making a phone call – maybe you're arranging a date, ordering some goods or asking a friend for some information. What sort of things do you say on the phone, that you don't say when you're talking to somebody face to face? There are a few useful phrases you need to know when talking on the phone in French so let's have a look at them now.

REMEMBER Be polite in the exam! Greet the examiner with **bonjour** when you go in, and say **au revoir** at the end.

67

◎ **Comment dit-on cela en français?** How do you say that in French?

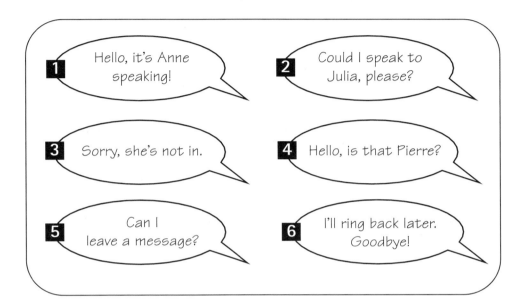

1 Hello, it's Anne speaking!

2 Could I speak to Julia, please?

3 Sorry, she's not in.

4 Hello, is that Pierre?

5 Can I leave a message?

6 I'll ring back later. Goodbye!

Practice questions

Can you answer this question?

> *Que penses-tu faire comme métier plus tard?*
> **Exemple:** *Je voudrais ...*

🎧 *Décris ton métier idéal.*

See how much you can remember!

Can you...

- name six jobs?
- ask what somebody wants to be?
- ask to speak to somebody on the phone?

Practice activity

Practise making phone calls in French by ringing people up! Ring a friend from your French class or a relation who speaks French and see what they've got to say for themselves – in French, of course!

The World of Work

Jobs vocabulary

◎ **Trouve les 12 métiers dans la grille.** Find the 12 jobs in the grid.

! REMEMBER Make yourself some learning cards to help you revise – write the 12 words from the wordsearch on pieces of card. Place them face down on a table. As you turn each card over, say a sentence or ask a question using that word.

◎ **C'est quel métier? Ecris le mot juste.** What job is it? Write the correct word.

1 On travaille dans une école. Il faut aimer les enfants pour faire ce métier.

....

2 Pour ce métier il faut travailler souvent pendant la nuit. On travaille dans un hôpital et on aide les malades.

....

3 C'est un emploi pour les gens qui adorent les voitures! On travaille dans un garage.

....

4 Cet emploi est très intéressant. On voyage tout le temps, mais on passe beaucoup de temps dans les aeroports. Il faut être poli avec les gens dans l'avion.

....

! REMEMBER If you can understand this text, but don't know the actual French word for the job, you can quickly look it up in a dictionary. Or if time's runing out, you'll just have to make a guess at what the word is – is it very similar to the English word?

ⓗ For extra writing practice, write your own definitions for jobs! Start with the 12 jobs in the wordsearch – or think of other jobs yourself. You can then give your definitions to a friend to work out.

Understanding job adverts

In the next activity, you'll be reading three short adverts. Don't worry if you don't understand every word! Read the instructions and the speech bubbles carefully - they'll help you to focus on what you're looking for.

 Before you do the activity, scan the texts for key words. Underline them. Can you see any similarities between any of the words in the speech bubbles and the words in the adverts? For example, **nature** might be connected to **jardin**. What other connections can you find?

> *Ma passion, c'est la nature. J'adore travailler en plein air. Je me lève très tôt, parce que je préfère travailler le matin.*

Virginie

> *Je suis l'aînée et il me faut garder mes petits frères. Ils ont trois et cinq ans. Le week-end je fais le babysitting pour les voisins. J'adore ça!*

Julie

> *Moi, j'aide beaucoup à la maison: je fais la cuisine, je nettoie ma chambre et de temps en temps je tonds la pelouse. Ça me plaît.*

Matthieu

1

On recherche:
jeune personne
(âge: minimum 18 ans)
pour nos deux filles adorables
(2 et 6 ans)
09h00–5h00 (juillet et août)
Contactez-nous au:
34 65 87 12

2

NOTRE HOTEL RECHERCHE:

(personnel ...)

▶ entre 16–25 ans
▶ pour travailler dans notre hôtel renommé
▶ juillet–octobre
▶ emploi varié!

✆ **65 78 95 45**

On recherche

une personne capable

pour nous aider dans notre jardin d'herbes aramatiques

7 heures par jour

(06h00 - 13h00)

Tel: 03 52 87 94 **3**

REMEMBER
You can scan texts to find information at a glance – this is especially useful when you don't need to answer detailed questions.

REMEMBER
You can write and scribble notes on the exam paper – it's not like a textbook in class!

The World of Work

◉ **Fais correspondre les jeunes gens aux petites annonces.** Match the young people to the adverts.

Virginie ☐   *Julie* ☐   *Matthieu* ☐

Did your underlined words help you do the activity?

Understanding forms

In your exam, you might be asked to understand a CV or you might have to produce one yourself. The personal details on this CV could also be useful if you had to fill in an ID form, an application form or leave your details at the lost property office.

◎ **Remplis le formulaire avec les détails ci-dessous.** Fill in the CV with the details below.

REMEMBER When you can copy French words in the activity, try not to make any careless mistakes with the spellings.

CURRICULUM VITAE

1 Nom: ....

2 Age: ....

3 Date de naissance: ....

4 Lieu de naissance: ....

5 Nationalité: ....

6 Père (nom/emploi): ....

7 Mère (nom/emploi): ....

8 Adresse (code postal): ....

9 Numéro de téléphone: ....

10 Formation: ....

11 Loisirs: ....

12 Emploi à temps partiel: ....

13 Emploi idéal: ....

REMEMBER Some words might be unknown to you – fill in the ones you're sure of first, then look at what's left over and try to make sensible guesses as to what goes on the other lines.

| ordinateurs/le cinéma | 18 | français |
| programmeur | Alain Dupont | Toulouse |

Herbert Dupont (journaliste)   distribue les journaux

Karine Dupont (comptable)   60.98.67.97

10, rue de Breil, 35051 Rennes   3 décembre 1981

1987–1992: l'école primaire à Toulouse;
de 1992: Lycée St.-Germain, Rennes

ⓗ Voluntary work

You'll probably get a longer text like the one below in the exam, especially at Higher level. You'll have to read and understand it so you can then do the activity. A good thing about reading French is that lots of French words look like their English equivalents!

⑦ Before you do the activity, underline all the words in the article that look like their English equivalents.

Aider les enfants de Rio, construire une école dans le désert, bien sûr, c'est passionnant. Mais pour faire du bien, il n'est pas nécessaire de voyager loin. Tout près de chez vous des dizaines d'associations cherchent des volontaires.

Des organisations célèbres comme **Médecins sans Frontières** reçoivent toujours beaucoup d'offres d'aide; leur problème c'est qu'ils ont surtout besoin de spécialistes (docteurs, technicien(ne)s, infirmiers et infirmières). Mais, dans toutes nos villes, des dizaines d'associations ont besoin de bénévoles comme vous.

Quelle association choisir?
Le centre national du volontariat peut vous aider à vous décider. Il faut parler de votre temps libre – et de vos préférences aussi. Et puis, si les hôpitaux vous rendent malade, il faut le dire!

Il n'est souvent pas nécessaire d'avoir une formation spéciale: les associations cherchent avant tout des personnes motivées et disponibles règulièrement.

Les enfants en difficulté
On recherche les volontaires pour aider les jeunes qui ont des difficultés scolaires ou pour les accompagner dans les sorties dans les musées, les parcs d'attractions, etc.

On recherche aussi des familles pour recevoir un enfant durant les vacances. Il existe aussi des associations qui s'occupent des enfants handicapés et des enfants mal traités.

Les adultes
Vous ne pouvez offrir que quelques heures par semaine? Il y a des associations qui aident les jeunes chômeurs à remplir des formulaires ou à se présenter pour un emploi. Ces associations cherchent également des volontaires pour aider ceux qui ont des difficultés à lire ou à écrire.

From Jeunes Francophones

❗ **REMEMBER** Use any headings of words in bold to help you understand and find your way around the article.

❗ **REMEMBER** The answers can often be lifted straight from the text, so don't spend too long thinking of new French words to use – they're probably already there!

ⓗ *Lis l'article et réponds aux questions.*

1 Qu'est-ce que les associations cherchent?
2 Médecins sans Frontières a besoin de qui?
3 Que fait le centre national du volontariat?
4 Quelles qualités doivent avoir les volontaires?
5 Qu'est-ce qu'on fait pour aider ceux qui ont des difficultés scolaires?
6 Quand est-ce que les enfants ont besoin d'une famille?
7 Comment peut-on aider les jeunes chômeurs?

Practice activity

Find your own French texts to read – you can look in your school textbook or ask your penfriend to send you some magazines from France. If you've got access to the internet, you'll be able to read lots of French. Just search for 'French' or 'France' or 'French magazines' and see where you end up! Or you can ask the BITESIZE internet team.

The World of Work

 # Writing

Focus on vocabulary for jobs

Your examiner has to be impressed that your French spelling is accurate. Test yourself in this first activity.

◎ **Ecris les mots.** Write down the words. They're all jobs.

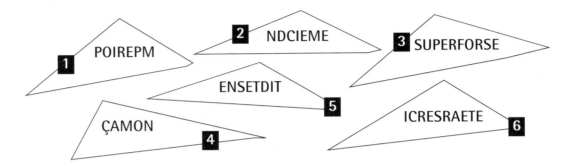

1 POIREPM
2 NDCIEME
3 SUPERFORSE
5 ENSETDIT
4 ÇAMON
6 ICRESRAETE

! R E M E M B E R
Make lists of useful vocabulary as you learn French – they'll help you revise for the exam.

◎ Look at the jobs in this table. Can you write down the missing male and female forms? You might need to use a dictionary.

MALE	FEMALE
le vendeur	la vendeuse
1 le facteur	
2	l'infirmière
3 le coiffeur	
4	l'ouvrière
5 le programmeur	
6	la directrice
7 l'employé de bureau	
8	la serveuse
9 le technicien	
10	la boulangère

Make sure that you check your answers in the back of the book. Make a note of any words you spelled wrong and try to learn them.

(?) What other jobs can you think of? Make a list of them.

Writing

Writing a CV

In a lot of writing activities, it's worth just thinking for a few moments before you actually put pen to paper. In this next activity, you need to think of suitable headings for a CV form. So, the first thing to do, is remember what a CV is! Then you can think of suitable headings. In this sort of activity, there is no 'correct' solution – as long as your headings are sensible choices, then you'll get marks. Obvious headings, of course, are things like your name, age and date of birth.

◎ **Ecris les titres pour le curriculum vitae.** Write the headings on the CV.

CURRICULUM VITAE

_____

_____

_____

_____

_____

_____

_____

_____

_____

_____

_____

_____

_____

_____

_____

! REMEMBER Always read the instruction carefully – here you only have to write the headings for the CV, so don't go and waste time filling it in with your details as well.

! REMEMBER Don't be put off when you see a great empty space that needs filling with French words! Just take your time to read the instructions, work out what you need to write, and then start filling in the space – bit by bit!

! REMEMBER Keep your writing neat at all times!

Check your headings against those on page 70 to see if they're the same.

◎ **Remplis le curriculum vitae avec tes détails.** Fill in the CV with your details.

The World of Work

Writing

Writing a text about yourself

The CV you filled in on page 73 used headings with brief bits of information – these provide a good starting point for writing a text all about yourself. You can take each line of information and write a full sentence on it – the more detail, the better! Once you've written sentences for all 13 headings, you'll have written a text. And that's what you'll need to do in the exam!

◎ **Ecris un texte sur toi-même.** Write a text about yourself.

Exemple:

Je m'appelle Juliette Blanc.
J'ai 17 ans. Je suis née le ..

74

 REMEMBER Think of things to write that you <u>do</u> know how to say. The exam is your opportunity to show what you do know – not what you don't know!

1 Nom:	Juliette Blanc
2 Age:	17
3 Date de naissance:	30 avril, 1981
4 Lieu de naissance:	Paris

Practice questions

Can you answer these questions – in writing?

Quels métiers aimes-tu? Pourquoi? _____

_____

Quels métiers n'aimes-tu pas? Pourquoi? _____

_____

Où est-ce que tu voudrais travailler? _____

h *Décris ton métier idéal.*

Practice activity

Check to see how much you know!

Can you...

- write down five jobs?
- write down six headings for a CV?

- write down four details about yourself?

ⓗ Exam focus: Writing a longer text

In the Higher writing exam, you'll be expected to write one piece of French of about 90–120 words. You might well have to write a letter (formal or informal) in which you'll need to include tenses, opinions and some description. Your task could be on any topic, and some exam boards give you a choice – **choisis A ou B**.

So let's have a look at the sort of choice you might get:

> **Choisissez A ou B. Ecrivez 120 mots.**
> **A** Vous avez passé une semaine idéale avec votre famille. Ecrivez une lettre à votre correspondante pour raconter ce que vous avez fait pendant cette semaine. Parlez de vos expériences et de vos impressions. Expliquez pourquoi la semaine était idéale.
>
> **B** Vous voulez faire un stage dans une compagnie française. Ecrivez une lettre à cette compagnie. Parlez:
> • de vous et de vos qualités personnelles
> • de vos passe-temps
> • de vos études au collège
> • des emplois que vous avez déjà faits.
> Expliquez pourquoi vous voulez faire ce stage.

On page 74, you saw one strategy for writing a longer text in the exam. But there are other ways of doing it as well. Here are a couple more ideas:

■ make notes – if you've got 100 words to write, then think of five headings to do with the topic area and write brief notes/key words under each. Then write your text out in full, padding your notes out to about 20 words on each heading.

■ if the question sets you tasks, work your way through the questions and headings in the actual question one by one, ticking them off as you go.

And what happens if you just can't get your piece of writing up to 100 words? Well, here are a few ideas:

■ include as many opinion phrases as you can (in the present and past tense):

> *... est/était formidable/génial.*
> *Je trouve/j'ai trouvé ... cool/super/affreux/dangereux/intéressant.*
> *... me plaît beaucoup/... m'a beaucoup plu.*

■ add details of time and place:

> *Ça s'est passé le week-end dernier.*
> *Je travaille à la banque entre huit et quatre heures – c'est fatigant.*

■ learn a few stock phrases for starting and finishing your text or letter:

> *Merci beaucoup pour ta lettre – elle était très intéressante.*
> *Et voici la fin de mon histoire bizarre!*

ⓗ *Choisis A ou B ci-dessus et écris une lettre.*

❗ R E M E M B E R
If you've got a choice of writing tasks, read them all through first. Then choose which piece of writing you want to do. There's no point choosing topic A and then deciding half-way through that you haven't got enough to write so you swap to B – there's no time for that!

❗ R E M E M B E R
To get top marks in the writing exam, you'll need to: do <u>all</u> of the tasks set; express opinions; give some descriptions; know how to start and end a letter; and use the present, past and future tenses accurately.

The World of Work

The International World

This section is about

- Countries

- Tourism

- The environment

This section is all about the international world and that includes the countries and places that you might visit, the hotel you might stay in or the train journey you might make. It's also about the environment and what people in French-speaking countries are doing to help it. These are all topics that you'll need to know about for your exam.

So what about you? How many countries have you visited? Have you been to many countries in Europe (**l'Europe**)? Or maybe you've been to America (**l'Amérique**), Africa (**l'Afrique**), Asia (**l'Asie**) or even as far away as Australia (**l'Australie**)!

Were you born in the country you now live in? If you were born in England, then you're probably English (**anglais(e)**), but if you were born in Scotland you'd be Scottish (**écossais(e)**). Do you know the words for Irish (**irlandais(e)**) and Welsh (**gallois(e)**)? Make sure you can say which country you live in and which country you were born in!

Lots of people move away from their own country and go somewhere else – they might go there on holiday, for business or to live and work. French speakers can go to a lot of countries and still understand everybody! Why's that? Well, French isn't just spoken in France (**en France**), Belgium (**en Belgique**) and

Switzerland (**en Suisse**) but it's also spoken in lots of African countries – these countries are known as **les pays francophones** (French-speaking countries). You probably know some of them already from the earlier programmes, but see how many countries you can see in this section.

One of the most important issues of the twentieth century is our environment (**l'environnement**) – and the harm we're doing to it. In the programme, you'll hear young people talking about the problems they see facing the environment and you'll also see an environmental project at work in Montreal. Are you worried about the environment? Maybe you're concerned about air pollution (**la pollution de l'air**) or perhaps it's tropical forests (**les fôrets tropicales**) that worry you.

So what do you do to help the environment? Maybe you recycle paper (**recycler le papier**) or perhaps you try to avoid waste altogether (**éviter le gaspillage**). Whatever you do, you're bound to get a good idea of what other people are doing around the world once you've watched the programme – you never know, it might even make you aware of some environmental issues you hadn't really thought about before!

So let's get started – **allons-y!**

◎ These phrases will be really useful for your exam, so see if you can try and learn them!

Countries

D'où viens-tu/venez-vous?
    Where do you come from?

Je viens de France/d'Angleterre ...
    I come from France/England ...

Je voudrais visiter l'Allemagne/la Belgique.
    I'd like to visit Germany/Belgium.

Je connais le Canada/la Suisse/l'Ecosse
    I know Canada/Switzerland/Scotland.

J'ai visité l'Espagne/la Grèce/l'Irlande.
    I've visited Spain/Greece/Ireland.

le Pays de Galles, les Pays Bas, l'Amérique
    Wales/The Netherlands/America

Quelle est ta nationalité?
    What nationality are you?

Je suis anglais(e)/français(e)/espagnol(e) ...
    I'm English/French/Spanish ...

russe, britannique, suisse, japonais(e)
    Russian, British, Swiss, Japanese

Tourism – Hotel bookings

Avez-vous des chambres libres?
    Have you got any rooms free?

Je voudrais une chambre avec douche.
    I'd like a room with a shower.

J'ai besoin d'une chambre pour une personne.
    I need a room for one person.

Est-ce qu'il y a un téléphone/une télévision dans la chambre?
    Is there a phone/television in the room?

Avec demi-pension ou pension complète?
    Half-board or full-board?

Pour combien de nuits?   How many nights?

Est-ce qu'il y a un parking?
    Is there a car park?

A quelle heure est le petit déjeuner?
    What time is breakfast?

Tourism – Train bookings

Un aller simple pour Nice, s'il vous plaît.
    A single ticket to Nice, please.

Un aller retour pour Toulouse.
    A return ticket to Toulouse.

Fumeur ou non-fumeur?
    Smoking or non-smoking?

Première ou deuxième classe?
    First or second class?

A quelle heure part le prochain train pour ...?
    When's the next train to ...?

Le train part de quel quai?
    What platform does it leave from?

Est-ce qu'il faut changer?
    Do I have to change?

Où se trouve la consigne/le guichet?
    Where's the left luggage/ticket office?

Le train est en retard.   The train is late.

The environment

Il faut recycler le verre/le carton/le papier ...
    You should recycle glass/card/paper ...

Il faut circuler à vélo..
    You should go by bike.

Il faut éviter le gaspillage.
    You should avoid waste.

Il faut acheter de l'essence sans plomb.
    You should buy lead-free petrol.

On ne faut pas polluer l'air.
    You shouldn't pollute the air.

Il faut éviter de faire des ordures.
    You shouldn't create rubbish.

Il faut jeter les papiers à la poubelle.
    You should throw paper in the bin.

La terre se réchauffe et il y a un trou dans la couche d'ozone.   The earth is heating up and there's a hole in the ozone layer.

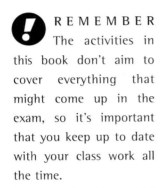

Listening

Ticking grids and filling forms

In the next activity you're going to tick a grid as you listen – this can be a bit tricky, as if you miss a number by mistake and think that you're listening to number 3 when in fact it's already number 4, then all your answers will be wrong, even if you understand the French, as you'll be ticking on the wrong line. You can avoid this by putting a blank piece of paper on the grid and each time the tape gives a number (**un**, **deux** etc.) you pull the paper down a line and tick on that line. Try it with this activity – just pull the paper down each time you hear a new voice.

REMEMBER The activities in this book don't aim to cover everything that might come up in the exam, so it's important that you keep up to date with your class work all the time.

Now find the clip where nine people answer the survey (**enquête**) question: **D'où venez-vous?** and do the activity.

Ecoute et coche la grille. Listen and tick the grid.

	Belgium	Italy	England	Germany	Canada	France	Switzerland
1							
2							
3							
4							
5							
6							
7							
8							
9							

Now listen again and check that you really have ticked the correct line each time – then you can check your answers at the back.

In the next activity, you're going to fill in a form as you listen. Check you understand all the headings on it first and know what sort of words you've got to write in the spaces. Then find the clip where Manuel talks about Hôtel Canella and do the activity.

REMEMBER Look out for words like **3 choses** in forms – that means that you've got to write three items – two items won't get you full marks and there's no need to list everything you hear – just <u>three</u> things.

Ecoute et remplis le formulaire. Listen and complete the form.

HOTEL CANELLE

1 Manuel: âge – ____________ **2** son père est: ____________

3 Combien de chambres: ____________

4 L'hôtel se trouve: ____________

5 Pour le petit déjeuner [3 choses]: ____________

6 Facilités à l'hôtel [4 choses]: ____________

____

ⓗ Answering questions on a longer passage

In this activity, you're going to listen to a report about an environmental project. It's longer than most of the clips you've worked on so far, but the reporter speaks very clearly and not too fast, so you should be able to do the activity. First of all read the questions below that you're going to have to answer. As always, they'll give you a clue as to the sort of things you might hear. You might like to look up a few words in the dictionary – but try to limit yourself to three at the most.

1 Qu'est-ce qu'il faut faire des déchets après le déjeuner?
2 La femme nomme quatre choses à mettre dans les poubelles. Lesquelles sont-elles?
3 Pourquoi la femme met-elle ces choses dans les poubelles?
4 Au dépôt il y a beaucoup de choses à recycler. Tu peux en nommer quatre?
5 Qu'est-ce qu'on fait des déchets organiques?
6 Ça dure combien de temps?
7 La femme parle avec l'homme: quelle proportion de déchets du collège est recyclable?
8 Pourquoi le recyclage, est-il important (selon l'homme)?
9 Où se trouve ce projet?
10 Pourquoi la ville a-t-elle la première «rue verte» du monde?

REMEMBER
If a question asks **où?** then you're listening out for a place for the answer and if it asks **combien?** then it's a number you need. It's very important that you know these question words (see page 3).

Now find the clip where the woman has just finished her lunch at the school canteen and do the activity.

◎ **Ecoute et réponds aux questions.** Listen and answer the questions (above).

You might like to listen through once and just make some notes for yourself here first:

REMEMBER
When you've got questions to answer on a passage, the questions are usually in the same order as the passage – so question 1 won't be about the end of the piece.

Practice activity

The video isn't your only chance of listening to French! Try to watch some programmes and adverts on a French cable or satellite channel. Or you could tune into a French radio station one evening a week and listen to a show. You could also ask your French penfriend or teacher to record some French programmes for you to listen to.

Speaking

Role play – at the hotel

In the exam, you'll probably be given a cue card for a role play. This will have pictures or symbols on – you need to use these for the conversation. The examiner will ask questions. You must look at the pictures and reply.

Let's start off with looking at some symbols you might find for a hotel role play. Your teacher might have more of these that you can copy and learn.

(?) See how many questions or sentences you can make up using the picture cues below.

REMEMBER
When you're revising you can make 'word spiders' like this one here on any topic you like. You can write useful words, phrases or questions on a topic – whatever you like!

Exemple:
– Je voudrais *une chambre pour une personne.*
– Avez-vous *des chambres libres?*
– J'ai besoin d'*une chambre avec une télévision.*

(?) Now have a go at answering these questions – they could be your examiner's script in the exam.

1 Est-ce que je peux vous aider?
2 Vous avez combien d'enfants?
3 Vous restez combien de nuits?
4 Avec salle de bains ou douche?
5 Demi pension ou pension complète?
6 Vous voulez autre chose?

REMEMBER
If the examiner asks you something like question 6 here – don't just reply **non**! Always try to think of something extra. For example, here you might ask if the room has a view, or what time breakfast is.

(◎) **Tu es à la réception. Complète la conversation.** You're at the reception desk. Do the role play. The examiner speaks first and your requirements are on the right.

1 Bonjour. Est-ce que je peux vous aider?
2 Pour combien de nuits?
3 Pardon?
4 Ça fait 600 francs.
5 Non, mais il y en a une dans la ville.
6 C'est entre six et dix heures.

1 a double room with a shower
2 four nights
3 respond by asking what it costs
4 ask if there's a pool in the hotel
5 ask when breakfast is
6 ask one more question

Role play – at the train station

If you get a role play at the station in the exam, there are a few key phrases that you'll need to have learned.

(?) Do you know how to ask for these things in French?

1 a single ticket
2 a return ticket (to Rouen)
3 what time the train leaves
4 a non-smoking carriage
5 what time the train arrives
6 which platform it goes from

Check your answers with the InfoZONE on page 77. Once you've practised those phrases and are familiar with them, you can put them into action. Have a go at this short role play at the station.

◎ **Tu es à la gare. Réponds aux questions.**
You're at the station. Answer the questions.

1 Bonjour Madame/Monsieur. Vous désirez?
2 Fumeur ou non-fumeur?
3 A quelle heure voulez-vous voyager?
4 Pardon?
5 67 francs. C'est tout?
6 Quai numéro quinze.

1 a single ticket to Nice
2 non-smoker
3 at 08.45
4 respond by asking how much it costs
5 yes, and ask which platform it goes from
6 say thank you and bye

! R E M E M B E R
If you're doing a role play at the hotel, station or the bank, for example, try and be polite and say **merci beaucoup** and **s'il vous plaît** to the person serving you!

In the exam, you'll probably get symbols rather than word cues, so here's another role play for you to practise some more.

⊕ *Tu es à la gare! Complète la conversation au guichet.*

Here's the examiner's part (he/she will begin):
1 Bonjour.
2 Vous désirez?
3 Bon, première ou deuxième classe?
4 Pardon?
5 120 francs.
6 Dans dix minutes. Quai numéro trois.

! R E M E M B E R
Practise asking the questions as well as giving the answers – you might need to ask questions in the exam!

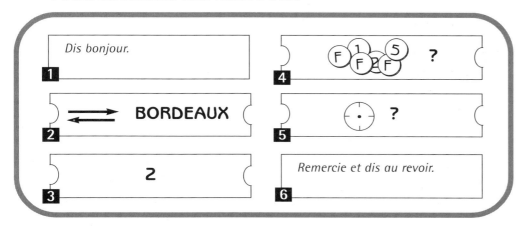

BITESIZEfrench

The Interntaional World

Speaking

Learning some stock phrases – environment

Before you go into the speaking exam, you won't know what topics the examiner is going to ask you about – and there's no way that you can know everything there is to say for every topic! It is important though that you try to learn a few phrases from each of the topics you cover in class.

Don't go for an overload when you're learning phrases as you're better off knowing three phrases accurately than ten phrases inaccurately or only half. Let's have a look at some stock phrases for the environment – and remember, you can use them in the writing exam as well!

> **REMEMBER** You can write five stock phrases for each topic and keep them in your revision folder. The InfoZONE pages in this book provide a good starting point for ideas.

> La terre se réchauffe – et ça c'est un grand problème.

> Nous polluons notre planète et je trouve ça effrayant.

> Des animaux sont menacés. C'est insupportable.

> Je m'inquiète parce qu'il y a un trou dans la couche d'ozone.

Phrases like **c'est un grand problème** (it's a big problem), **je trouve ça effrayant** (I find that frightening), **c'est insupportable** (it's unbearable) and **je m'inquiète** (I'm worried) can be used for topics other than the environment – so they're doubly worth learning!

Practice questions

Can you answer these questions?

> *Bienvenue à notre hôtel. Vous désirez?*
> **Exemple:** *Je voudrais …*
> *Pour combien de nuits?*
> **Exemple:** *Pour …*

h *Imagine une conversation à l'aéroport.*

See how much you can remember!

Can you...

- ask five questions at a hotel?
- ask four questions at a station?
- say three things about the environment?

Practice activity

Work with a friend from your French class and make up little dialogues together – you can use any situation you like, such as in a shop or at the station/airport. Record your dialogues on to tape and play them back – do you sound 'French'? Could you improve your dialogues by adding more expression or using a variety of words or maybe making your sentences longer? Try again until you're both happy with your recording. Put your finalised recording in your French revision folder to revise from again nearer the exam.

Exam focus: strategies for the oral exam

Q: "What do I do if I'm in the oral exam and I don't understand the examiner?"

A: You say **Comment?** or **Pardon, mais je ne comprends pas** or **Est-ce que vous pouvez répéter, s'il vous plaît?** or **Pouvez-vous parler plus lentement, s'il vous plaît?**

Q: "What do I do if I'm in the oral exam and I can't remember a word I need?"

A: You try to avoid that word and say something else. The examiner doesn't know what word you were thinking of in the first place, so as long as you can come up with a suitable alternative, you'll get a mark. For example, if you can't remember how to say 'I was born in Spain but I live in England', you can say **Je viens de Madrid, mais j'habite Manchester.**

Q: "What do I do if I'm in the oral exam and I need some extra time to think about my answer?"

A: Use some French-sounding 'filler' words. Here are some examples. Try saying them now and make yourself sound as French as possible!

Bein ...   Alors ...   Un moment ...   Euh ...   Je réfléchis ...

Q: "What do I do if I'm in the oral exam and I just can't think of anything further to say on a topic?"

A: Give your opinion! Say what you think or thought about something **Je trouve/j'ai trouvé ça ...** or ask the examiner a question! **Et vous? Avez-vous vu ce film? Comment trouvez-vous la musique jazz?**

Q: "What do I do if I'm in the oral exam and I don't understand a picture on the role play cue card?"

A: Ask the examiner to explain it – in French, of course! **Excusez-moi, mais que signifie ce dessin? Je ne le comprends pas.**

Q: "What do I do if I'm in the oral exam and I realise I've just said something that's completely wrong?"

A: Don't panic! Just say **Ah, je m'excuse! Ça n'est pas correct. Je veux dire ...** and then go on to correct yourself.

! REMEMBER In the oral exam, you'll be recorded on to tape, so don't be put off by the sound of the tape going round!

! REMEMBER Go into the oral exam with some key phrases in your memory – it's up to you then to make sure you use those phrases in your exam.

! REMEMBER The examiner won't be trying to catch you out in the exam – he or she will want you to score as many marks as possible, so try and relax and answer the questions clearly and to the best of your ability.

●●●● Reading

Map of European countries

The exam won't test you on your geographical knowledge like this next activity, but you can use this map to help you revise – once you're done the activity, cover up the French words and see how many of the countries you can name.

◎ **Trouve chaque pays sur la carte.** Find each country on the map.

1 *l'Allemagne*
2 *la France*
3 *l'Autriche*
4 *l'Espagne*
5 *la Grande-Bretagne*
6 *la Suisse*
7 *l'Italie*
8 *la Belgique*

1e							

❗ **REMEMBER** Match all the countries you're sure of first and cross them out in pencil as you do so. Then go back over the other ones and try to work out the full answer.

❔ Can you name any of the other countries on this map?

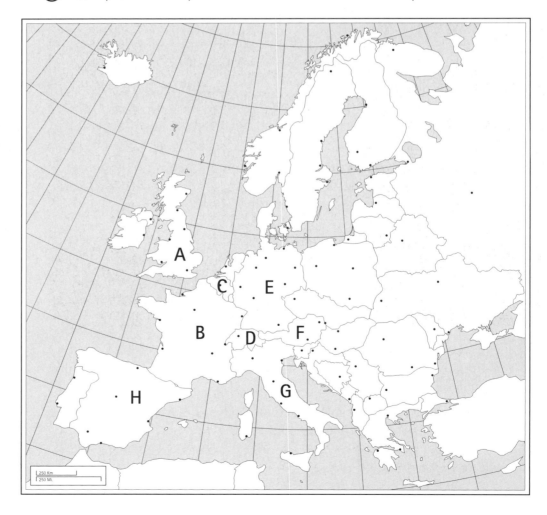

Looking at signs and photos

In the exam, you might get photos or pictures of signs and notices to read – and answer questions about. You won't always understand every word, but that doesn't matter, as it's the key words you need. You can, of course, look up any unfamiliar words in the dictionary, but you haven't got a lot of time, so you'll have to choose those words carefully.

(?) Look at these signs. Can you work out where you'd find each one? How did you work out where they'd be? Which words helped you?

! R E M E M B E R
If a question is only worth one mark, then there's probably not much point looking up lots of words for that question. Concentrate more on the questions that are worth three or four marks if you're going to look words up.

! R E M E M B E R
Write important French words down when you do activities here or in your textbook. Keep them in your French revision folder so you can revise them again before the exam.

◎ **C'est quelle photo?** Which photo is it?

1 Un aller retour pour Nice, s'il vous plaît.
2 Je voudrais deux tartes aux fraises et une baguette.
3 Avez-vous des saucissons?
4 Le centre-ville? Prenez la première rue à droite.
5 Est-ce que je peux parler au docteur?
6 Deux crêpes à la confiture, s'il vous plaît.

Understanding French handwriting

In the next two activities you're going to read some handwritten messages. In the exam you'll be given a variety of texts to read and these might include handwritten letters and postcards – just like these ones!

(?) First of all, just look at this postcard. Can you read all the words? Are there any words that are hard to read? Underline them.

Chère Geneviève !
Je suis en Amérique ! Je prends des cours d'anglais. Le temps est magni- fique. Il y a du soleil chaque jour et je bronze ! Le matin je vais à l'école de langues et j'y suis des cours pendant trois heures. C'est dûr ! Les autres étudiants sont sympas et ils viennent du monde entier. D'Amérique du Sud, de Suisse, d'Australie. Je suis le seul français. Vendredi je suis allé à une fête chez une copine, c'était super, et le weekend dernier, nous sommes allés à Disneyworld.
À bientôt !
Matthieu.

Geneviève Martin
17 Boulevard Wilson
Bordeaux 33100
FRANCE

! REMEMBER
Don't be put off by handwritten texts – you just need to look a little harder to work out the words.

◎ Can you find these words in the postcard? Write them down.

1 lesson ....   4 students ....
2 sun ....   5 party ....
3 every ....   6 soon ....

Compare your handwriting with the words on the postcard. Do they look the same? Have you written the accents on properly? Is your handwriting easier to read than that on the postcard?

◎ **Lis la carte postale. Vrai ou faux?** Read the postcard. True or false?

	vrai	faux
1 Matthieu est en Amérique.	☐	☐
2 Il apprend à jouer au tennis.	☐	☐
3 Il fait beau.	☐	☐
4 Les étudiants sont tous américains.	☐	☐
5 Matthieu vient de France.	☐	☐
6 Il va visiter Disneyland demain.	☐	☐

h *Lis la lettre et réponds aux questions ci-dessous.*

> Chère Sharon,　　　　Québec, le 5 juin
>
> Merci de ta lettre. C'est toujours avec plaisir que je te lis.
>
> En ce moment je suis très occupée car je viens de m'inscrire, à mon école, à un groupe qui travaille sur l'environnement. Le projet dont nous faisons partie s'intéresse au recyclage. Aussi avons-nous plein de poubelles spéciales recyclage. Maintenant tous les élèves trient leurs détritus. Il y a des poubelles pour les piles électriques, le papier, le carton, les canettes en aluminium et il y en a même pour les déchets organiques (ces derniers proviennent de la cantine). Notre groupe est responsable des poubelles et quand elles sont pleines, nous les emportons dans la cour de l'école. Tous les soirs un camion passe les ramasser. La plupart des élèves sont très sérieux et jettent leurs déchets dans les poubelles spéciales. Le mardi c'est mon tour d'aider à nettoyer la cour de l'école. Et à ton école y a-t-il un système semblable?
>
> Écris-moi vite pour me raconter.
> À bientôt　Amicalement
> Anna

1 Pourquoi Anna est-elle très occupée en ce moment?
2 Le projet s'intéresse à quoi?
3 D'où viennent les déchets organiques?
4 Qu'est-ce que le groupe d'Anna fait des poubelles?
5 Quand est-ce que le camion ramasse les poubelles?
6 Qu'est-ce qu'Anna fait le mardi?

Now look at your handwritten answers to the questions. Is your writing neat and easy to understand? Will the examiner know what you've written? Show them to a friend and check that he or she can read them!

! REMEMBER Make sure you learn the question words:

que? – what?
qui? – who?
où? – where?
comment? – how?
quand? – when?
pourquoi? – why?
quel(le)? – which?

Practice activity

If you've got a French penfriend, ask him or her to send you handwritten letters – not ones typed on a computer! He or she could also send you a photocopy of some pages from his/her exercise books for you to read. See how much of it you can understand!

If you haven't got a penfriend, ask your teacher or French assistant if they could get you some photocopies of pages from French exercise books – the more you look at French handwriting, the easier it will be to understand in the exam!

Writing

Focus on vocabulary for countries

◎ **Où se trouve ces destinations? Ecris les noms des pays.** Where are these destinations? Write down the names of the countries.

88

a LONDRES
b GENÈVE
c BRUXELLES
d VIENNE
e QUÉBEC
f BRETAGNE
g SÉVILLE
h LISBONNE
i MOSCOU

! R E M E M B E R
Some towns are spelled differently in French. Try to get them right if you write them in the exam!

....
....
....
....
....
....
....
....

? What other countries can you think of? Make a list of them.

◎ **Regarde le graphique. Quelle est la nationalité des personnes au collège international?** Look at the chart. What nationality are the people at the international college?

Exemple:
113 personnes sont françaises.
Il y a 113 personnes françaises.

! R E M E M B E R
Make lists of useful vocabulary as you learn French – they'll help you revise for the exam.

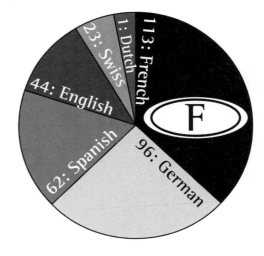

113: French
1: Dutch
23: Swiss
44: English
62: Spanish
96: German
F

Make sure that you check your answers in the back of the book. Make a note of any words you spelled wrong and try to learn them.

Writing a hotel booking letter

In the exam you might be asked to write a hotel booking letter. No need to panic though, as this page will take you through a possible formula. First of all, look at this sample letter.

89

> Hôtel du Pont
> 34, rue Ravel
> 79308 Niort
>
> Cannes, le 4 mai
>
> Monsieur,
>
> J'ai l'intention d'aller à Niort en avril. J'arriverai le 5 avril et j'aimerais rester jusqu'au 8 avril. Je vais assister au grand congrès au centre-ville. Je voudrais réserver une chambre pour une personne pour trois nuits. Je préférérais une chambre avec salle de bains. J'arriverai en voiture et j'aimerais bien réserver aussi une place dans votre parking.
>
> Je vous prie d'agréer, Monsieur, l'expression de mes sentiments distingués.
>
> H. Baptiste

REMEMBER If the exam paper doesn't provide you with an address to write on your letter, don't spend ages making one up – just write Paris or Nice or any other French town.

OK, so what's the formula there? Look at the five points below and underline the corresponding text in the letter:

1 write your address and the date
2 write the address of the person you're writing to
3 start with a greeting (see page 90)
4 write your request
5 sign off (see page 90).

Now you can have a go at writing your own letter – just fill in the numbered blanks with your own information.

Ecris une lettre à l'hôtel. Write a letter to the hotel.

REMEMBER In the exam you'll probably be told what you need to ask for in a letter like this – here you can just practise by asking for a double room with a shower for two nights.

2 _____
1 _____
3 _____
4 _____
5 _____

The International World

BITESIZEfrench

Writing

Tips for writing a letter

In the exam you may well have to write a letter. There are a few things you should remember.

- always write the place and the date on the top right-hand side of the letter: **Strasbourg, le 4 mai**

- begin your letter **Cher (Monsieur) ...**, to a male, **Chère (Madame) ...**, to a female and **Monsieur/Madame ...** if it's a business letter and you don't know the person's name

- end your letter **A bientôt** or **Ecris-moi bientôt** or if it's an informal letter

- end your letter **Je vous prie d'agréer, Madame/Monsieur, l'expression de mes sentiments distingués** if it's a formal letter

A: Ecris une lettre à ton ami(e). Explique tout ce que tu fais pour protéger l'environnement. OU
B: Tu es en vacances en Australie. Ecris une lettre à ton/ta correspondant(e). Explique tout ce que tu fais et décris le pays un peu.

REMEMBER If you're not sure about how to do an activity or you've got a question you'd like to ask someone about your French revision, then you can contact the BITESIZE team on the internet. The e-mail address is on the back of this book.

Practice questions

Can you answer these questions – in writing?

Quels pays as-tu visités? Quand?

Tu aimerais visiter quels pays? Pourquoi?

Quelle est ta nationalité?

Décris des vacances idéales.
Ecris une lettre au «Grand Hôtel» pour réserver des chambres pour ta famille.

Practice activity

Check to see how much you know!

Can you...

- write down five countries?

- write down six nationalities?

- write down four things you might write in a letter?

📺 In the video, there were several phrases with the word **de** that used verbs in their infinitive form (see page 35). These sorts of phrases are worth learning as they can be very useful. Do you remember hearing this one?

> *Ça permet de communiquer avec le monde.*

There are more phrases which follow that pattern and you might remember hearing them in the other programmes or on the tapes from your school course book. Let's a have a look at some:

J'ai envie de *parler le français.*	I want to speak French.
Il décide d'*aller en Suisse.*	He decides to travel to Switzerland.
Elle essaie de *réserver une chambre.*	She's trying to book a room.
Je suis en train d'*apprendre l'anglais.*	I'm in the process of learning English.

◎ Fill in the gaps – you can use any infinitive verb you like as long as it makes sense!

1 J'ai envie de ....
2 Nous avons décidé de ....
3 Mes copains essaient de ....
4 Je suis en train de ....
5 Vous avez envie d' ....?
6 Le train. Ça permet de ....

Don't forget that verb endings change when they're not in the infinitive! For example, you say **j'ai envie** (I want) but **vous avez envie** (you want). You'll find the pattern for **avoir** and **être** on page 35, but verbs like **essayer** (to try) are also irregular. You can probably get more information about irregular verbs from the back of your course book – or ask your teacher to recommend a grammar book for you.

📺 In the video, there were also some phrases that use an infinitive without **de**. Look at these examples:

> *Il faut nettoyer les rues.*   *Il ne faut pas créer des ordures.*

There are more phrases which follow that pattern and they're often connected with wanting to do something. Let's have a look at some important ones:

Je voudrais *demeurer en Australie.*	I'd like to live in Australia.
Il aime *voyager par le train.*	He likes travelling by train.
Nous voulons *sauver la planète.*	We want to save the planet.
Est-ce que **tu peux** *réserver une chambre?*	Can you book a room?
On doit *recycler le papier.*	You should recycle paper.

◎ Write these sentences in French.

1 I'd like to visit Canada.
2 We can recycle paper and batteries.
3 You should put bottles in the special bins.
4 The children shouldn't go to school by car.
5 They want to build a new road.
6 You like protecting the environment.

Answers

Everyday Activities

📺 Listening

Page 10

Popular subjects: *la biologie (twice), l'anglais, les sciences naturelles, la musique, le français, les mathématiques, le sport, les sciences physiques*

Disliked subjects: *l'anglais (twice), les mathématiques (twice)*

Page 11

Teachers: *1e, 2a, 3c, 4b, 5d, 6f*

Transport (1): *1c, 2a, 3a/d, 4 d/a, 5 b/a/c, 6 b/d/a*

Transport (2): *1d, 2d, 3c, 4a, 5e, 6a/d*

Page 12

Julien's room: *le salon – 1, 3, 7, 8, 10; la chambre de Julien – 2, 5, 6, 11*

Julien's routine: *a) se réveille, b) sept heures dix, c) salle de bains, d) trente, e) petit-déjeuner, f) tartines, g) chocolat chaud, h) huit, i) quitte*

Page 13

Parts of the body: *f, c, a, h, e, g, b, d*

Speaking

Page 14

Timetable questions: *1 le sport, 2 l'informatique, 3 la biologie, 4 les maths, 5 la chimie*

Page 15

Clock times: *Il est … a) douze heures et quart, b) trois heures moins cinq, c) huit heures et demie, d) onze heures cinq, e) huit heures vingt, f) dix heures dix, g) quatre heures moins le quart, h) une heure*

Reading

Page 18

Wordsearch: *pomme, poulet, œuf, pain, poisson, chocolat, jambon, thé, biscuit, soupe, café, croissant*

Odd word out: *1 les devoirs, 2 la côtelette, 3 la musique, 4 affreux, 5 la maison, 6 le dentifrice, 7 le train*

Page 19

Daily routine sentences: *b, c, f, g, a, d, e*

Questions and answers: *1c, 2f, 3d, 4e, 5a, 6b*

Sentence halves: *1e, 2d, 3b, 4f, 5c, 6a*

Page 20

Menus: *Jean – 3, Tim – 1, Katherine – 2*

Page 21

Dialogues: *Chez Clémentine – f, d, e, a, c, b A la pharmacie – g, e, d, c, f/h, b, i, a, f/h*

Writing

Page 22

Subjects: *1 maths, 2 sciences, 3 anglais, 4 français, 5 géographie*

Food list: *1 côtelette, 2 pommes de terre, 3 beurre, 4 pain, 5 eau, 6 pommes, 7 vin, 8 sucre*

Page 23

Andy's text: *Je m'appelle Andy. J'habite Leeds. Je me réveille à huit heures et demie. Je mange un croissant pour le petit-déjeuner. Je bois une tasse de café. Je vais à l'école en vélo. Ma matière préférée, c'est la chimie. Je n'aime pas le français.*

Page 24

Transport sentences: *Dix personnes vont à pied. Huit personnes vont en autobus. Sept personnes vont en métro. Cinq personnes vont par le train. Trois personnes vont en voiture. Deux personnes vont en vélo. Une personne va par le tram.*

GrammarZONE

Page 25

Le/la lists: *le café, le professeur la viande, le beurre, la tartine, l'école (f)*

The/some: *le – du, la – de la, l' – de l', les – des*

Gap filling: *1 du poisson, 2 des frites, 3 du chocolat chaud, 4 de la limonade, 5 des biscottes*

Personal Life

 ## Listening

Page 28
Brothers and sisters: *1d, 2c, 3c, 4c, 5d, 6a, 7d, 8a/c, 9e*

Ages: *1 cinq (5), 2 trois (3) et sept (7), 3 seize (16) et trois (3), 4 seize (16), 5 huit et demi (8.5), 6 dix (10), 7 quinze (15), 8 vingt-trois (23)*

Page 29
Forms: *Mère – Chantal, Age – 43, Travail – à la bibliothèque, Adore – les mots-croisés, Caractère – un peu snob*
Frère – Emile, Age – 11, Caractère – mignon, Adore – le foot, Aime le plus – les rats, A combien – 40
Père – Travail – à la poste, Passe-temps – jouer aux boules, aller au café, Caractère – très gentil

Questions: *1 à la bibliothèque, 2 43, 3 une tasse de thé, 4 le petit frère de Clémentine, 5 les photos de ses joueurs préférés, 6 ses rats, 7 le père de Clémentine, 8 6h30 (à six heures trente), 9 ses amis, 10 oui, elle adore son père*

Page 30
Sports grid: *1e, 2d, 3b/c/f, 4c, 5c, 6a/f/h, 7f/g*

Page 31
Birthday dates: *1 le 23 avril, 2 le 16 juin, 3 le 13 mai, 4 le 27 septembre, 5 le 10 mai, 6 le 28 octobre, 7 le 15 octobre, 8 le 23 octobre*

Countries: *1 l'Allemagne, 2 Amérique du Sud/Pérou, 3 Canada, 4 Russie*

Speaking

Page 32
Second dialogue: *C'est le seize juin. J'ai dix-sept ans. Oui, j'ai une sœur. Elle s'appelle Roz. Et j'ai un frère. Il s'appelle Steve. Je reçois deux livres chaque semaine. Je fais des jeux-vidéos et je fais de la natation.*

GrammarZONE

Page 35
Gaps: *1 manger, 2 faire, 3 aller, 4 danser, 5 lire*

Verbs: *écouter – j'écoute, tu écoutes, il/elle écoute, nous écoutons, vous écoutez, ils/elles écoutent*
habiter – j'habite, tu habites, il/elle habite, nous habitons, vous habitez, ils/elles habitent

Reading

Page 36
Wordsnake: *oncle, mère, frère, sœur, père, tante, cousin(e)*

Hobbies: *1b, 2d, 3e, 4c, 5a*

Countries: *1 Italie, 2 Allemagne, 3 Espagne, 4 FRANCE*

Page 37
Photo: *vrai – 2; faux – 1, 3, 4; je ne sais pas – 5*

Newspaper article: *vrai – 2, 4, 5; faux – 1, 3, 6*

Page 38
Rouen leaflet: *1 faire du sport – natation, 2 s'installer dans la salle technologique, 3 faire les activités au centre des jeunes – la photographie, 4 visiter le zoo*

Page 39
Comprehension questions: *les enfants et jeunes (jusqu'à 16 ans), 2 dans la salle technologique, 3 chaque lundi (à 10h00), 4 en autobus ou par le train, 5 (any two) la photographie, dessiner, faire la cuisine, danser, 6 43.23.43.56, 7 non*

Writing

Page 40
Sports: *a) du basket, b) du vélo, c) du ski, d) du football, e) du tennis de table, f) de la natation, g) de la voile, h) du tennis*

Questions: *1 Où habites-tu? 2 Où travaille ta mère? 3 Quel âge as-tu? 4 Comment t'appelles-tu? 5 Quelle est la date de ton anniversaire? 6 Est-ce que tu as des frères ou des sœurs?*

Page 41
ID form: *1 surname, 2 first name, 3 address (with postcode), 4 nationality, 5 age, 6 date of birth, 7 hair, 8 eyes, 9 height, 10 hobbies*

Page 43
Gaps for 'train': *1 le train, 2 j'entraîne, 3 traîne, 4 il forme/instruit*

The World Around Us

📺 Listening

Page 46
Places in town: *les magasins, un marché, deux statues, un temple, un port, un cinéma, une place, les cafés, une cathédrale*

Dijon tick boxes: *1, 4, 5, 6, 8*

Page 47
Directions (1): *map b is correct (road opposite, first road on the left, straight on and it's at the end of the road)*

Directions (2): *place 5 is correct (go across the bridge, go right, go straight on, get to the square and it's opposite)*

Page 48
Multiple choice – shopping: *1b, 2a, 3c, 4c, 5c, 6a, 7b, 8a*

Page 49
Numbers 1–20: *un, deux, trois, quatre, cinq, six, sept, huit, neuf, dix, onze, douze, treize, quatorze, quinze, seize, dix-sept, dix-huit, dix-neuf, vingt*

Numbers 21–99: *21 vingt et un, 44 quarante-quatre, 22 vingt-deux, 33 trente-trois, 70 soixante-dix, 80 quatre-vingts, 66 soixante-six, 88 quatre-vingt-huit, 90 quatre-vingt-dix, 55 cinquante-cinq*

Speaking

Page 50
Places in town: *1 un théâtre, 2 une gare, 3 un cinéma, 4 un musée, 5 un hôpital, 6 un château, 7 des magasins, 8 une piscine*

Page 51
Places in town: *1 la poste, 2 l'université, 3 le métro, 4 le supermarché, 5 le stade, 6 la mairie*

Direction pictures: *1 Tournez à gauche. 2 Allez tout droit. 3 Tournez à droite. 4 Prenez la deuxième rue à droite. 5 Allez jusqu'à la gare. 6 Prenez la première rue à droite.*

Page 52
Shopping list items: *1 une bouteille d'eau minérale, 2 une tarte aux cerises, 3 quatre baguettes, 4 des pommes de terre, 5 cinq tomates, 6 du café, 7 un poulet, 8 du jambon*

GrammarZONE

Page 53
Words from box: *1 rouges, 2 grande, 3 bleu, 4 petits*

Gap filling: *1 vieille, 2 beau, 3 bons, 4 affreuses*

Reading

Page 54
Direction pictures: *1 turn right, 2 turn left, 3 carry straight on, 4 cross the bridge, 5 opposite the church, 6 next to the bank*

En ville puzzle: *1 piscine, 2 banque, 3 service, 4 magasin, 5 hôpital, 6 bibliothèque, 7 gare*

Page 55
Weather forecast: *1c, 2b, 3a, 4e, 5f, 6h, 7g, 8d*

Speech bubbles: *6, 4, 7, 3, 8, 2, 5, 1*

Page 56
Places in town symbols: *1b, 2e, 3g, 4d, 5f, 6a, 7h, 8c*

Questions: *1 Valognes, 2 il joue au football, 3 il va à la pêche, 4 les magasins et les cafés, 5 en banlieue, 6 elle est très vieille, 7 elle s'est cassée la jambe*

Page 57
Shopping brochure: *1 côtelette de porc et des saucissons, 2 un yaourt aux fruits et du beurre de Normandie, 3 haricots verts, 4 tartes aux fraises et un yaourt aux fruits*

Writing

Page 58
Clothes: (clockwise from top) *jupe, chaussures, blouson, robe, chemise, pantalon*

Directions: *Tu vas à gauche et puis tu prends la première rue à droite. Tu continues tout droit. Tu prends la deuxième rue à droite et tu vas jusqu'aux feux. Là tu vas à droite et ma maison se trouve dans cette rue à droite.*

The World of Work

📺 Listening

Page 62
The five jobs: *1 professeur, 2 médecin, 3 conducteur de train, 4 au chômage, 5 banquier*

Times: *1 08:00, 2 08:00, 3 08:30, 4 07:00, 5 16:40, 6 19:00, 7 22:00*

Page 63
Matching jobs to reasons: *a2, b4, c3, d5, e1*

Gaps in sentences: *1 j'aime, 2 aime/bien, 3 un contact, 4 toute de la vie, 5 intéresse*

Page 64
Multiple choice – adverts: *1a, 2c, 3c, 4b, 5b*

GrammarZONE

Page 65
Tu/vous: *1 vous, 2 vous, 3 tu, 4 tu, 5 tu, 6 vous*

My, your, his/her: *1 mon/ma, 2 sa, 3 ta, 4 son*

Our, your, their: *1 vos, 2 notre, 3 leurs, 5 leur*

Speaking

Page 67
Phone phrases: *1 Allô. C'est Anne à l'appareil. 2 Est-ce que je peux parler à Julia, s'il vous plaît? 3 Je suis désolé(e), mais elle n'est pas là. 4 Allô, Pierre? 5 Est-ce que je peux laisser un message? 6 Je rappellerai plus tard. Au revoir.*

Reading

Page 68
Jobs wordsearch: *serveur, patron, ouvrier, maçon, professeur, vétérinaire, médecin, gendarme, fermier, pilote, chef, dentiste*

Job descriptions: *1 professeur, 2 infirmier/infirmière (docteur), 3 mécanicien(ne), 4 steward/hôtesse de l'air*

Page 69
Job adverts: *Virginie – 3, Julie – 1, Matthieu – 2*

Page 70
CV: *1 Alain Dupont, 2 18, 3 3 décembre 1981, 4 Toulouse, 5 français, 6 Herbert Dupont (journaliste), 7 Karine Dupont (comptable), 8 10, rue de Breil, 35051 Rennes, 9 60.98.67.97, 10 1987–1992: l'école primaire à Toulouse; de 1992: Lycée St.-Germain, Rennes, 11 ordinateurs/le cinéma, 12 distribue les journaux, 13 programmeur*

Page 71
Voluntary work: *1 les volontaires, 2 les spécialistes, 3 il vous aide à décider, 4 motivé et disponible régulièrement, 5 on les accompagne pour les sorties dans les musées, les parcs d'attractions etc., 6 pendant les vacances, 7 on peut les aider à remplir des formulaires ou à se présenter pour un emploi*

Writing

Page 72
Jobs: *1 pompier, 2 médecin, 3 professeur, 4 maçon, 5 dentiste, 6 secrétaire*

Male/female forms: *1 la factrice, 2 l'infirmier, 3 la coiffeuse, 4 l'ouvrier, 5 la programmeuse, 6 le directeur, 7 l'employée de bureau, 8 le serveur, 9 la technicienne, 10 le boulanger*

The International World

📺 Listening

Page 78
Grid: *1 France, 2 France, 3 France, 4 Germany, 5 Belgium, 6 England, 7 Italy, 8 Canada, 9 Switzerland*

Form: *1 13 ans, 2 directeur de l'hôtel, 3 150, 4 au bord de la plage, 5 (any three) fruit, pain, yaourts, fromage, jambon, 6 (any four) la piscine, la mer, les boules, le club de voile, la plage, le club pour les enfants, le restaurant, le bateau, les îles*

Page 79
Comprehension questions: *1 les mettre dans les poubelles spéciales, 2 l'aluminium, les bouteilles de verre, le plastique, les déchets organiques, 3 parce qu'ils sont recyclables, 4 (any four) papier, boîtes en carton, bouteilles en verre, cannettes en aliminium, plastique, piles, 5 du composte, 6 un mois, 7 90%, 8 parce que nous préservons une résource, 9 à Montréal, 10 parce que tous les marchants participent au projet du recyclage*

Speaking

Page 80
Hotel reception role play: *1 Bonjour. Je voudrais une chambre avec une douche. 2 Pour quatre nuits. 3 Ça coûte combien? 4 Est-ce qu'il y a une piscine dans l'hôtel? 5 Le petit déjeuner, c'est à quelle heure? 6 (examples) Avez-vous un parking? Est-ce qu'il y a un jardin pour les enfants? On peut jouer au tennis ici?*

Page 81
Train station role play (1): *1 Un aller simple pour Nice, s'il vous plaît. 2 Non-fumeur. 3 A neuf heures moins le quart (huit heures quarante-cinq). 4 Ça coûte combien? 5 Oui. Le train part de quel quai? 6 Merci. Au revoir.*

Train station role play (2): *1 Bonjour. 2 Un aller retour pour Bordeaux, s'il vous plaît. 3 Deuxième classe, s'il vous plaît. 4 Ça coûte combien? 5 A quelle heure part le train? 6 Merci beaucoup. Au revoir.*

Reading

Page 84
Countries: *1e, 2b, 3f, 4h, 5a, 6d, 7g, 8c*

Page 85
Signs and photos: *1g, 2b, 3h, 4c, 5d, 6a*

Page 86
Words from the postcard: *1 cours, 2 soleil, 3 chaque, 4 étudiants, 5 fête, 6 bientôt*

True/false: *vrai – 1, 3, 5; faux – 2, 4, 6*

Page 87
Questions on letter: *1 parce qu'elle vient de s'inscrire à un groupe qui travaille sur l'environnement, 2 au recyclage, 3 de la cantine, 4 il les emporte dans la cour de l'école quand elles sont pleines, 5 tous les soirs, 6 elle aide à nettoyer la cour de l'école*

Writing

Page 88
Countries: *a) l'Angleterre/la Grande-Bretagne, b) la Suisse, c) la Belgique, d) l'Autriche, e) le Canada, f) la France, g) l'Espagne, h) le Portugal, i) la Russie*

Pie chart: *113 personnes sont françaises. 96 personnes sont allemandes. 62 personnes sont espagnoles. 44 personnes sont anglaises. 23 personnes sont suisses. Une personne est hollandaise.*

GrammarZONE

Page 91
Sentences: *1 Je voudrais visiter le Canada. 2 Nous pouvons recycler le papier et les piles. 3 Vous devez mettre les bouteilles dans les poubelles spéciaux. 4 Les enfants ne doivent pas aller à l'école en voiture. 5 Ils veulent construire une nouvelle rue. 6 Tu aimes protéger l'environnement.*